Language Development Activity Book

with Standardized Test Practice

8

Scott Foresman

ESL

Accelerating English Language Learning

Authors

Anna Uhl Chamot
Jim Cummins
Carolyn Kessler
J. Michael O'Malley
Lily Wong Fillmore

Consultant

George González

Longman

ISBN 0-13-028548-X

Pearson Education
10 Bank Street, White Plains, NY 10606

45678910—CRK—05040302

Contents

Name ______________________________

Comparisons

Maria
Age 13
5 feet tall

Selena
Age 16
5 feet, 6 inches tall

Antonio
Age 10
4 feet tall

Maria and her brother and sister are always comparing themselves. Study the information under the pictures. Then complete the comparisons.

Age

1. Maria is younger than Selena.
2. Maria is __________ Antonio.
3. Antonio is __________ Maria.
4. Antonio is __________ Selena.

Size

5. Selena is taller than Maria.
6. Antonio is __________ Selena.
7. Selena is __________ Antonio.
8. Maria is __________ Selena and __________ Antonio.

Now compare yourself to two friends or family members.

Age

I am ______________________________

I am ______________________________

Size

____

____

Name ____________________

What are your traits?

Complete the paragraphs with the words from the box. You may use each word more than once.

has	have	is	are

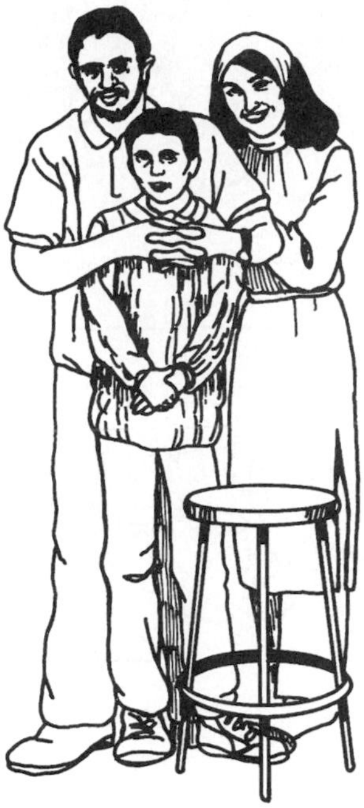

You ____________ certain traits. Your height, your hair color, and your eye color ____________ all traits. Another trait ____________ the age at which you get your growth spurt.

You and your parents probably ____________ many of the same traits. For example, if your parents ____________ dark hair, you probably ____________ dark hair. And if your parents ____________ short, you probably ____________ short. If your father ____________ blue eyes, you may have blue eyes, too. If your mother ____________ thin, you may be thin too.

Your traits ____________ determined by your genes. Genes ____________ passed from parent to child. Half your genes ____________ from your mother and half ____________ from your father. This mixture determines your traits. The passing of genes from parents to children ____________ called heredity.

Name ____________________

What are you buying?

Write the plural names of these things that you can buy in a grocery store.

egg	grape	tortilla
tomato	cherry	strawberry
carrot	cookie	apple

1. 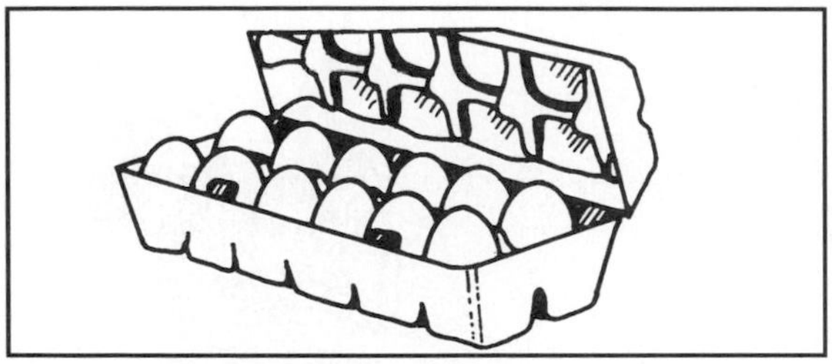

eggs

2. 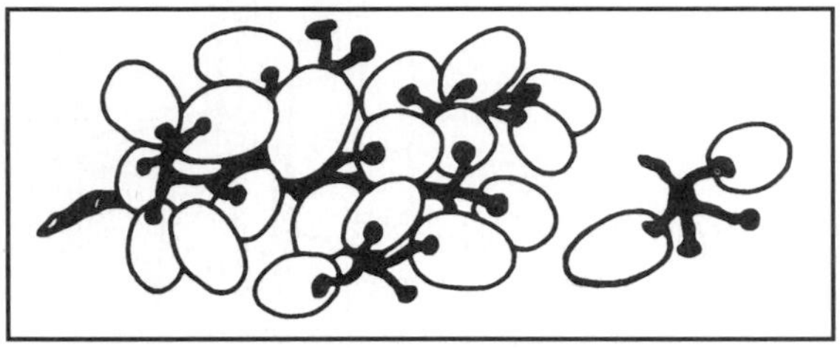

____

3. 

____

4. 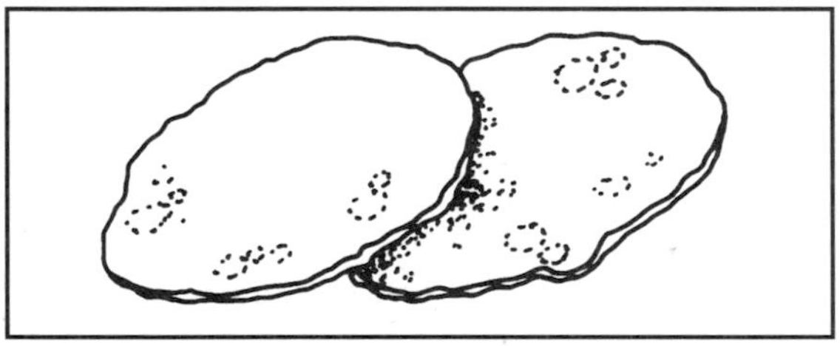

____

5. 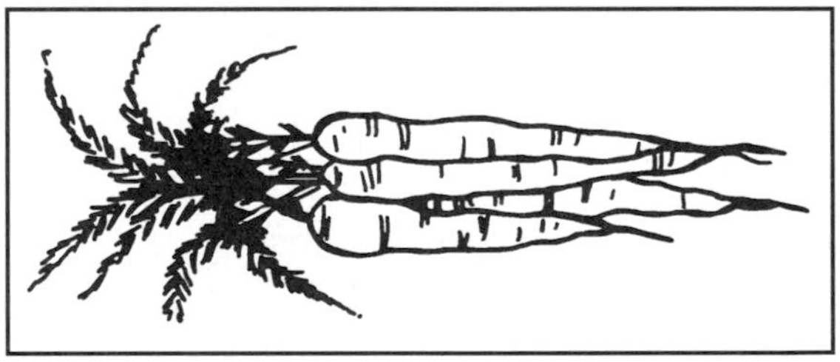

____

6. 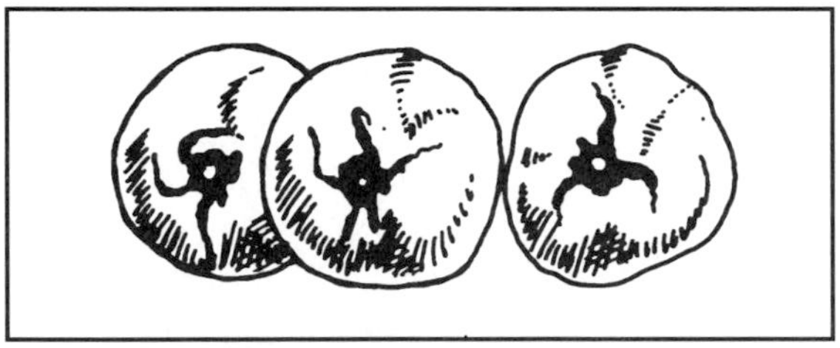

____

7. 

____

8. 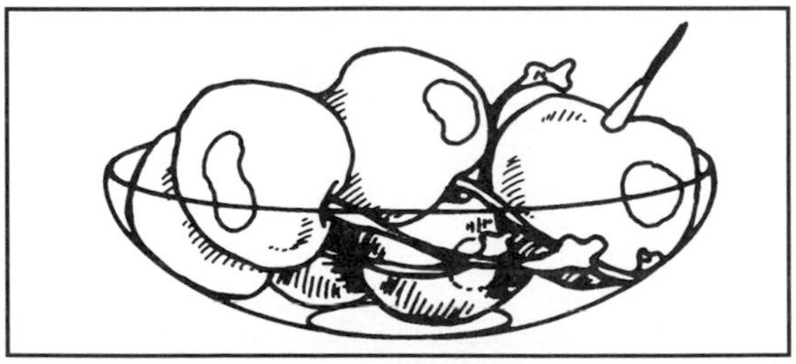

____

9. 

____

Name ______________________________

Which food group is it?

Place each food in the correct food group.

Foods				
bananas	bread	butter	candy	cheese
chicken	eggs	fish	lettuce	milk
nuts	onions	orange juice	pears	rice
spinach	strawberries	toast	tortillas	yogurt

Food Groups

Grains

____
____
____
____
____

Fruits

bananas
____
____
____
____

Dairy Products

____
____
____
____

Vegetables

____
____
____
____
____

Meat, Poultry, and Related Foods

____
____
____
____
____

Fats, Oils, Sweets

____
____
____
____

Name ______________________________

My Favorite Foods

List your ten favorite foods. Then write each one in the correct part of the food pyramid.

1. ______________________ 2. ______________________

3. ______________________ 4. ______________________

5. ______________________ 6. ______________________

7. ______________________ 8. ______________________

9. ______________________ 10. ______________________

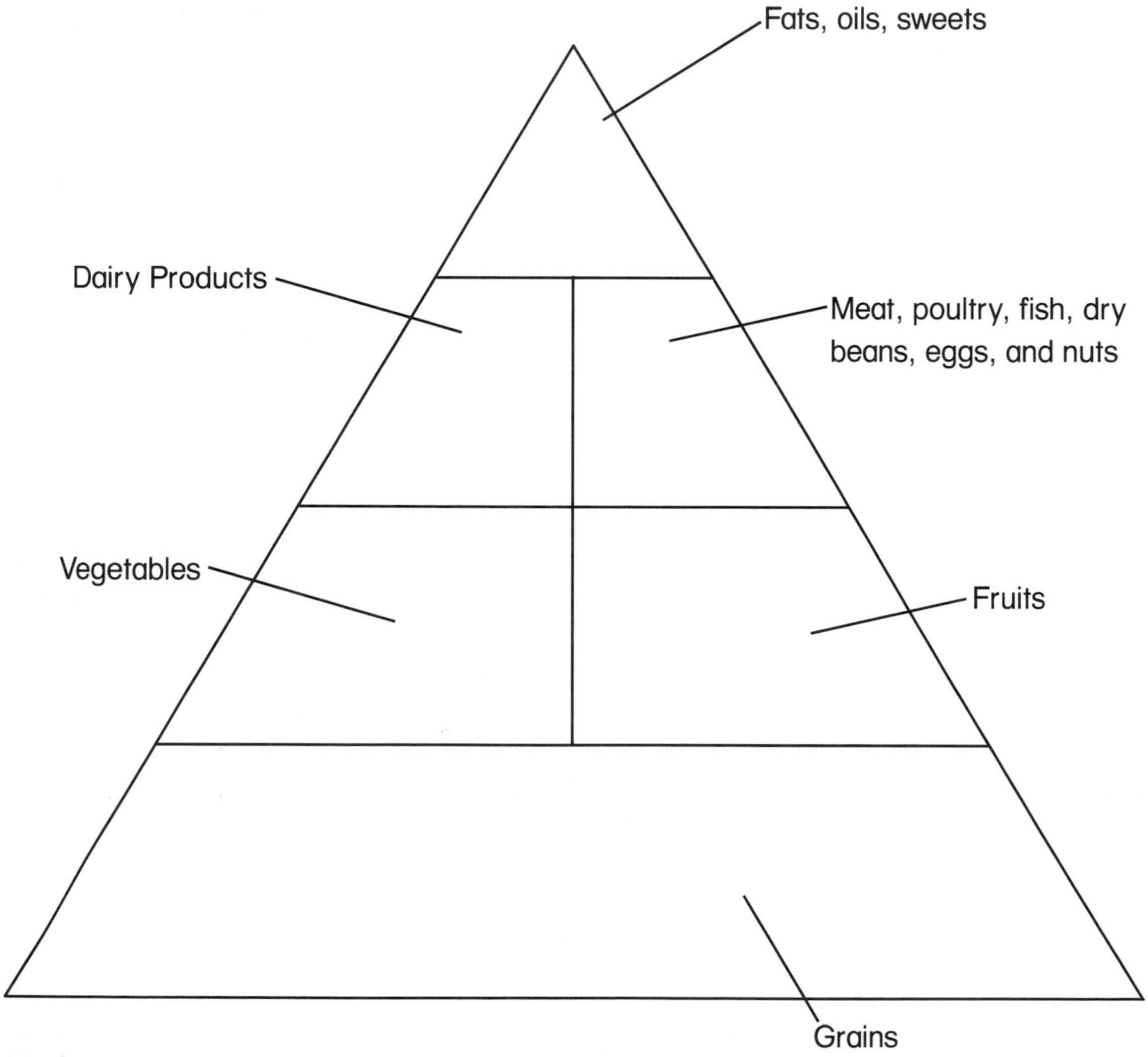

Name ______________________________

Measuring with Our Feet

Work with a partner to measure things. Place the heel of one foot directly in front of the toes of the other foot. Count each step as a "foot." Write your answers in the chart. Are your numbers different from those of your partner?

Measuring with Our Feet		
How Many Feet Long Is . . .?	Using My Feet	Using My Partner's Feet
The Teacher's Desk		
The Longest Classroom Wall		
A Hall in My School		
The Playground or Athletic Field		

Name ____________________

World Records

Write a headline for each story. Be sure to use the superlative in each headline.
Watch out! Where are most of these foods on the food pyramid?

1. The Largest Pie

Glynn Christian baked an apple pie that was bigger than any that had ever been baked before. The pie weighed 30,115 pounds.

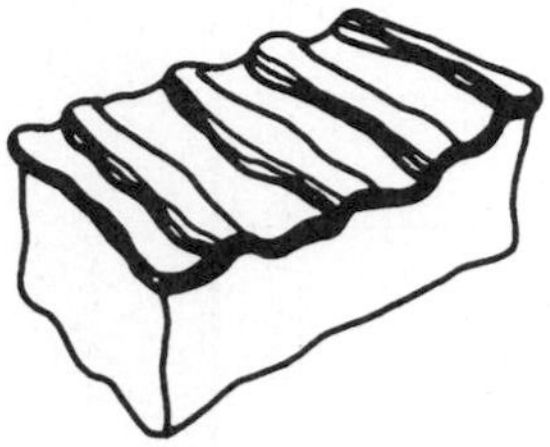

2. ____________________

A museum in Switzerland has a cake that is older than any other cake in the world. It was found in a tomb in Egypt and was baked over 4,000 years ago.

3. ____________________

Some people in Pennsylvania created a banana split that was longer than any other. It was 4.55 miles long.

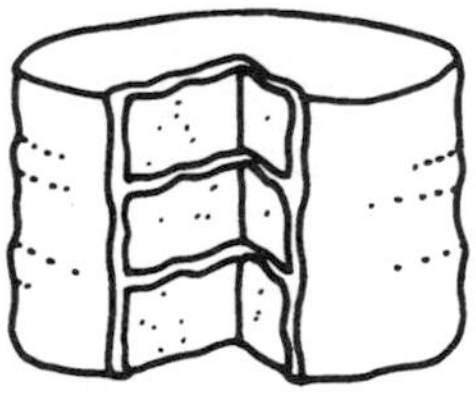

4. ____________________

Beth Cornell and her helpers built a cake that was taller than any other. It was 101 feet, 2 1/2 inches tall and had 100 layers.

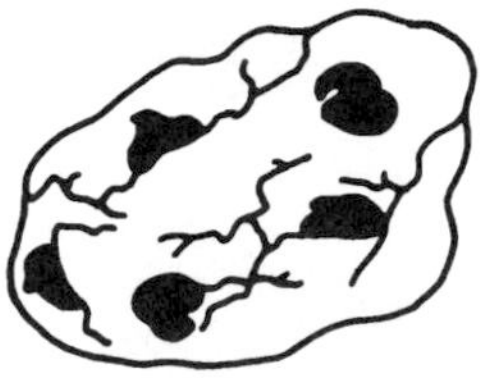

5. ____________________

The people of Ripon, Wisconsin, baked a cookie that was larger than any other. It contained 600 pounds of sugar and almost 4 million chocolate chips.

6. ____________________

Some people in California built a burrito that was longer than any other. It was over 2,000 feet long and contained 738.5 pounds of tortillas.

Name ______________________________

Opposites

Draw lines to connect each word in the first column with its opposite in the second column.

Words	Opposites
1. big	slow
2. young	night
3. bottom	sell
4. laugh	short
5. day	end
6. in front of	small
7. begin	top
8. fast	cry
9. tall	old
10. buy	in back of

Complete the sentences. Use words in the opposites list.

1. The foods you should eat a lot of are at the ____________ of the pyramid.
   The foods you should eat very little of are at the ____________ of the pyramid.

2. Girls often ____________ their growth spurt at the age of 9.
   Boys often ____________ their growth spurt at the age of 11.

Name ______________________________

Math Objectives: Demonstrate an understanding of measurement concepts using metric and customary units.

Express or solve problems using mathematical representation.

Clues

1. When you take tests, do not forget to use the formula chart in the test for all measurement conversions and formulas.
2. Be careful when you read questions that consist of charts, graphs, and Venn diagrams. Use a highlighter to mark important information in the question and/or the graph.

Samples

1. Babies are weighed in pounds and ounces and adults are weighed in pounds. If an adult weighs 142 pounds, what is this amount equal to in ounces?
   A. 158 ounces
   B. 852 ounces
   C. 2,272 ounces
   D. 4,394 ounces

Using a formula chart, you will see the conversion:
1 pound = 16 ounces

So multiply 142 (number of pounds) by 16 (number of ounces in a pound).
The correct answer choice is C.

2. There are 152 eighth-graders at Pallo Junior High. They are all taking electives. Some students are taking more than one elective. For example, 20 students are taking both band and art. Some students are taking just one elective. For example, 48 students are taking just band.

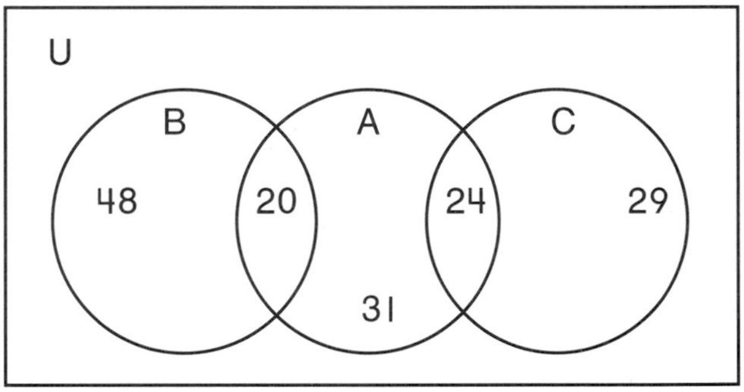

U = set of 152 students
B = set of band students
A = set of art students
C = set of choir students

How many students in this junior high do *not* take band *or* choir?

A. 75
B. 55
C. 51
D. 44
E. 31

The correct answer is E.

Name ______________________________

Try It

Read each problem. Mark the circle next to the correct answer.

1. Lily made a long-distance call to her sister in Mexico City. The first minute cost her $1.25 and each additional minute cost $0.45. If Maria talked for 6 minutes, which number sentence could be used to find C, the cost of her long-distance phone call?

   - ○ C = 6($1.25) + $0.45
   - ○ C = $1.25 + 5($0.45)
   - ○ C = 6($1.25 + $0.45)
   - ○ C = 6($1.25 - $0.45)
   - ○ C = 6($1.25) + $0.90

2. *The Guinness Book of Records* says that the tallest man stood 8 feet 11 inches. What would his height be in inches?

   - ○ 54 inches
   - ○ 81 inches
   - ○ 96 inches
   - ○ 107 inches

3. The bar graph represents the number of push-ups 5 students completed during a physical fitness test.

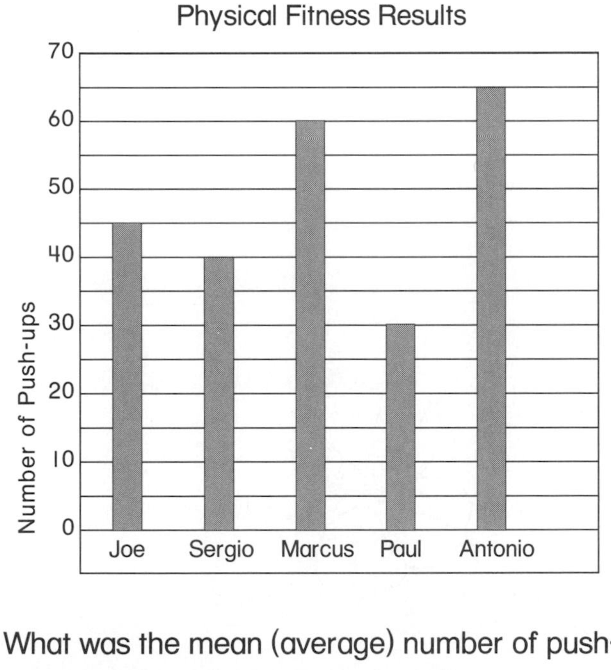

What was the mean (average) number of push-ups completed by the 5 students?

   - ○ 28
   - ○ 32
   - ○ 40
   - ○ 44
   - ○ 48

4. Sonny is saving to buy a new bike. It will cost $187.45, including tax. He saved $30 in June and $45 in July. Which equation could be used to find A, the amount of money he has left to save?

   - ○ $30 + $45 - $187.45 = A
   - ○ $187.45 - $30 - $45 = A
   - ○ $187.45 + $30 - $45 = A
   - ○ $187.45 - $30 + $45 = A
   - ○ $30 + $45 + $187.45 = A

Name ______________________________

The Parts of a Plant

Label the parts of the flower. Use the words in the box.

petal	leaf	stamen
pistil	stem	

Write sentences that describe the flowers. Choose from the words in the box or use words of your own.

curved	large	straight	wide
small	narrow	pointed	

1. ______________________________

2. ______________________________

Name ______________________________

Animals, Insects, and Plants

Finish the words. Use *p, pl,* or *pr.*

Animals and insects __pl__ay an important role in the life of ______ants. Bees and other insects help ______ants ______ollinate. They carry ______ollen from the stamens of a ______ant to the ______istils. The wind may also carry ______ollen from one ______ant to another.

After ______ollination, the flower dries up and falls off. Now the ______ant ______oduces seeds. The seeds might fall to the ground. The wind or animals might carry them to another ______ace. The seeds then grow into new ______ants. The new ______ants ______oduce flowers. And the cycle of the ______ant repeats itself.

Create an imaginary flower. Draw a picture of it and describe it.

Name ____________________

The Plants I Eat

Think of the plant parts you eat during one week. Write the name of each plant part in the correct column of the chart.

The Plant Parts I Eat Every Day						
	Seeds	Stems	Leaves	Flowers	Roots	Fruits
Monday						
Tuesday						
Wednesday						
Thursday						
Friday						
Saturday						
Sunday						

Answer the questions.

1. Which category of plant part do you eat most often? ____________________

2. Which category of plant part do you eat least often? ____________________

3. What is your favorite plant part? ____________________

Name ______________________________

What did Mike buy?

Mike just returned from the grocery store. The things he bought are on the table. What did he buy?

Mike bought these things:

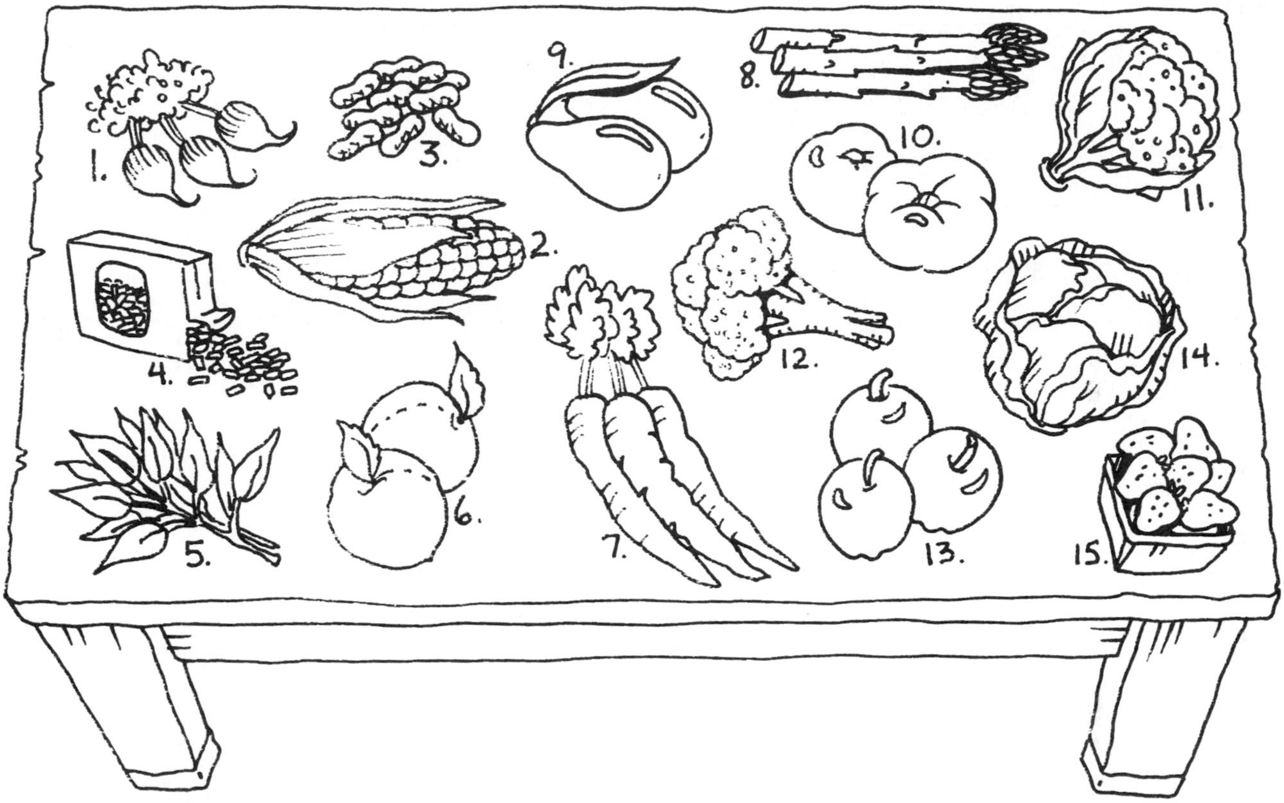

1. radishes
2. ______________
3. ______________
4. ______________
5. ______________
6. ______________
7. ______________
8. ______________
9. ______________
10. ______________
11. ______________
12. ______________
13. ______________
14. ______________
15. ______________

Name ______________________________

Where is the bee?

Tell where the bee is in each picture. Choose from the words in the box.
Use each word only once.

above	below	inside
at the bottom of	in front of	on top of

1.

The bee is ____below____ the flower.

2.

The bee is ______________ the flower.

3.

The bee is ______________ the plant.

4.

The bee is ______________ the flower.

5.

The bee is ______________ the plant.

6.

The bee is ______________ the flower.

Name ______________________________

Find the patterns.

Complete the following series with numbers or letters.

1. 1, 2, 4, 7, 11, 16, 22, 29, ________
2. 1, 3, 2, 4, 3, 5, 4, 6, 5, ________
3. 1, 2, 3, 6, 7, 14, 15, 30, ________
4. 5, 10, 12, 24, 26, 52, 54, ________
5. 3, 7, 11, 15, 19, ________
6. 4, 7, 10, 8, 11, 14, 12, 15, 18, 16, ________
7. A, C, E, G, I, K, ________
8. Z, W, T, Q, N, ________

Complete the following patterns.

1.

2.

3.

Make some patterns of your own. Give them to a friend to complete.

Name ______________________________

Why?

Form sentences by drawing lines to connect one choice from column 1 with one choice from column 2. Each sentence should tell why something happened in "The Story of Johnny Appleseed." Use each choice only once.

1. It was lonely making America
2. Apple trees are beautiful
3. Jonathan Chapman never threw an apple core away
4. The child in Pennsylvania was crying
5. The child stopped crying
6. Jonathan decided to pick the seeds out of the apple mash
7. The men laughed at Jonathan and called him Johnny Appleseed
8. Johnny Appleseed was a friend to birds, beasts, and humans

because he wanted to plant apple trees across the West.

because he never carried a gun and left wonderful apple trees wherever he went.

because they thought his plan was silly.

because he loved apple trees.

because they have blossoms in the spring and apples in the fall.

because it was such a big country.

because Jonathan promised to plant apple trees where the child was going.

because he didn't want to leave the apple trees.

Name ______________________________

Crossword Puzzle

Complete the puzzle.

Across

2. they cover and protect the flower buds until the flowers open
5. underground parts of a plant
7. they protect the parts of the flower that make seeds
8. opposite of *below*
9. opposite of *top*
10. opposite of *wide*
13. opposite of *above*

Down

1. it is carried by bees from plant to plant
2. they make pollen
3. it makes and holds the egg cells
4. opposite of *curved*
6. they grow into plants
7. combining of pollen with eggs to produce seeds
11. opposite of *narrow*
12. opposite of *bottom*

Name ____________________

Reading Objective: Determine the meanings of words in a variety of texts.

Science Objective: Demonstrate the ability to sequence, order, and/or classify scientific data.

Clues

1. Meanings of words can be determined by knowing the meaning of prefixes (added to the beginning of words) or suffixes (added to the end of words). It is important to remember that prefixes and suffixes change the meaning of the word.
2. Context clues can be found within the sentence where the word appears. The clues can also be in the sentence before or in the sentence after.
3. When you take tests, some questions may ask you to classify scientific information or events according to similarities and differences. Reread the passage to make sure you have selected the best choice.
4. Sometimes you are asked to put some material in sequential order. This means to arrange events in the order in which they happened.

Samples

Plants grow in many sizes and shapes. When you want to grow a plant, you begin by planting a seed. After a few days or weeks, the seed will germinate. As the tiny roots appear from the seed, the new plant also forms a stem. The roots grow down and the stem grows up, where leaves and flowers develop.

1. The first thing you do when you grow a plant is to
   A. get some dirt
   B. water it
   C. plant a seed
   D. pollinate it

To answer question 1, look back at the passage. The passage says that the first thing to do is to "plant a seed."

2. You can tell from the passage that *germinate* means
   A. begin to grow
   B. form a stem
   C. form a leaf
   D. turn green

If you look back in the passage, you can figure out that *germinate* means "begin to grow." Both forming a stem and forming a leaf are part of growing, but they are not the first steps.

Name ______________________________

Try It

Read the passage carefully. Mark the circle next to the correct answer for each question.

Plants

Flowers and leaves are two important parts of plants. Flowers help the plants reproduce. Pollen grains combine with the eggs in a flower to produce seeds. Leaves help plants produce food. The leaves of some plants grow in Fibonacci sequences. This series of numbers was named after Leonardo Fibonacci, who developed the series. The series starts with two 1s. Each number following is the sum of the two numbers before it.

Fibonacci Sequence
1
1 (0 + 1)
2 (1 +1)
3 (2 + 1)
5 (3 + 2)
8 (5 + 3)
? (8 + 5)
? (? + 8)

1. What sum shows what comes after 5 in the Fibonacci Sequence?

   ○ (5 + 3)

   ○ (1 + 1)

   ○ (? + 3)

   ○ (2 + 3)

2. In the chart above, what number should come next in the sequence

   2, 3, 5, 8, ?

   ○ 16

   ○ 12

   ○ 14

   ○ 13

Name ______________________________

Air Masses

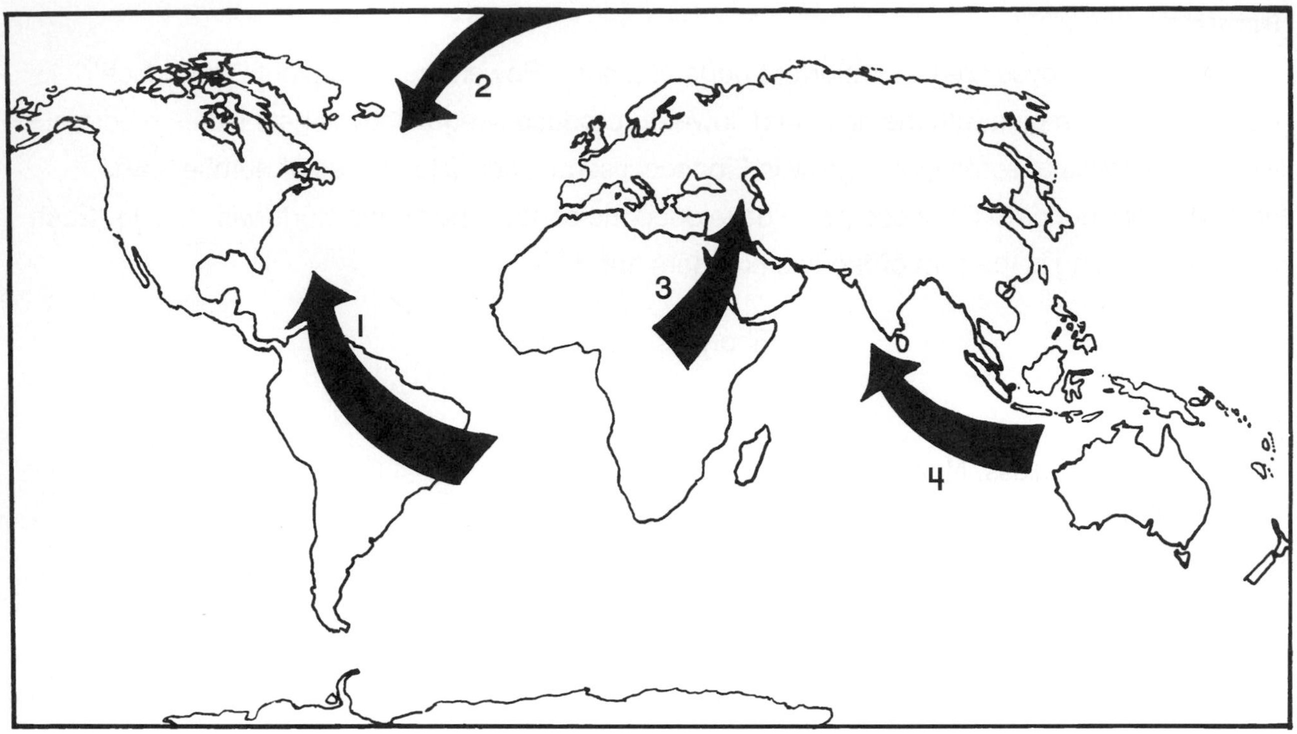

Describe each air mass on the map. Choose from the following combinations. You may use a choice more than once.

hot and dry	cold and dry
hot and humid	cold and humid

1. hot and humid
2. ______________________________
3. ______________________________
4. ______________________________

Now draw an air mass on the map over the area where you live. What kind of air mass is it most likely to be?

____

Name ______________________________

An Amazing Air Trick

Read the following story.

Yesterday our science teacher, Ms. Fujima, showed us a surprising trick. She used only a sink, a drinking glass, and a paper towel.

First, she filled the sink with water. Next, she crumpled the paper towel into a ball. She pushed the paper towel into the bottom of the glass. Next, she turned the glass upside down and pushed it straight into the sink of water. Then she lifted the glass straight out of the water. When she was done, we studied the results.

What a surprise! The paper towel stayed dry. Ms. Fujima explained that there was air in the glass. The air took up space and kept the water from going into the glass. So the towel did not get wet.

Now rewrite the second paragraph as a numbered list of steps.

Things you need: a sink, a drinking glass, a paper towel

Follow these steps:

1. ____Fill____ the sink with water.
2. ______________ the paper towel into a ball.
3. ______________ the paper towel into the bottom of the glass.
4. ______________________________
5. ______________________________
6. ______________________________

Name ______________________________

Describing a Process

Describe what is happening in the pictures. Use the correct forms of the words in the box. You may use some words more than once.

fall	form	push	rise

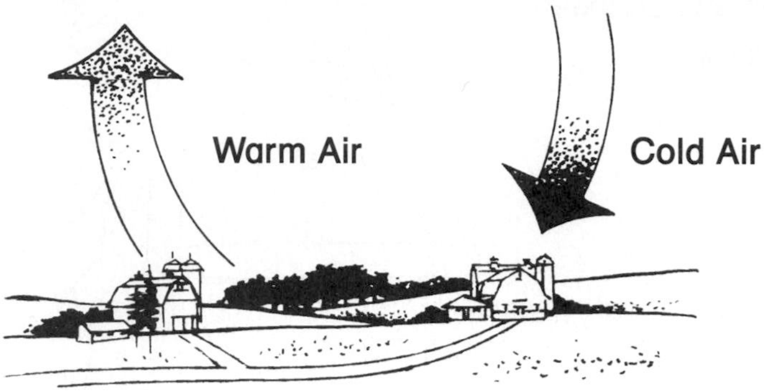

1. Warm air ____rises____.

2. Cold air ______________ down.

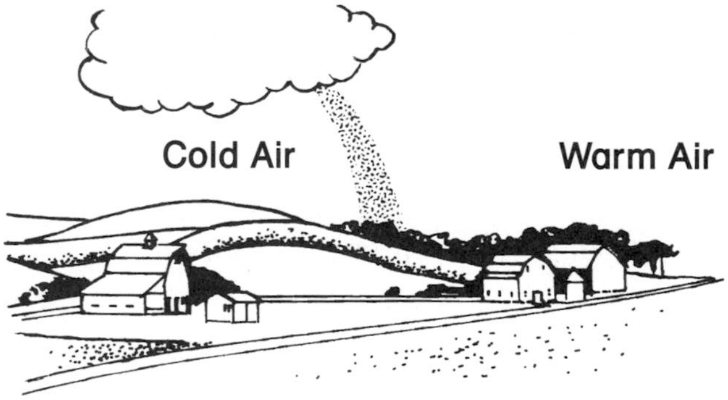

3. A front ______________ where two different air masses meet.

4. The cold air mass ______________ into the warm air mass.

5. The warm air ______________ very fast.

6. Water in the air ______________ clouds.

7. Then the water ______________ to the earth as rain.

Name ______________________________

Weather Words

Rewrite the sentences using words that end in *-y.*

1. In San Francisco, there is often a lot of fog.
   In San Francisco, it is often foggy.
2. At the top of a high mountain, there is often snow.
   At the top of a high mountain, it is often ________.
3. Where two different air masses meet, there may be a storm.
   Where two different air masses meet, it may be ________.
4. When warm air rises and cools, the sky fills with clouds.
   When warm air rises and cools, the sky becomes ________.
5. Do you prefer a day when the sun shines or a day when it rains?
   Do you prefer a ________ day or a ________ day?

Here are four new idioms with weather words. Can you guess what they mean by studying the words around them? Draw a line from each idiom to its meaning. (Hint: A breeze is a soft wind.)

1. Marta has such a **sunny** personality. She's always happy and in a good mood.
2. Luis **is snowed under.** He has two tests tomorrow and he has to help the science teacher after school.
3. Kim studied hard every day, so she thought the English test was **a breeze.**
4. Stan is very shy. When he goes to a party where he doesn't know many people, he finds it hard to **break the ice.**

easy

talk to people he doesn't know

has a lot of work to do

cheerful

Name ____

A Husband for the Princess

Fill in the blanks to tell the story of Princess Mi Noung. Use the pronouns in the box.

he	she	they

Princess Mi Noung was sad. __________ was growing old, and __________ didn't have a husband. Her father, the Emperor, did not like any of her suitors. __________ wanted Mi Noung to marry a powerful person.

Then one day two suitors came to the palace. __________ both wanted to marry Mi Noung. The Emperor liked them both. __________ told them to bring gifts for Mi Noung.

The two suitors left quickly. The Spirit of the Sea went back to the ocean. __________ got pearls and fish for Mi Noung. The Spirit of the Mountain went back to the mountain. __________ got jewels and fruit for Mi Noung.

Who would marry the Princess?

Name ______________________________

The Battle of the Spirits

Finish telling the story of Princess Mi Noung by filling in the missing words. Use the correct past tense forms of the verbs in parentheses.

The next morning ____came____ (come). The Spirit of the Mountain ______________ (arrive) first. He ______________ (show) his gifts. The Emperor ______________ (like) the gifts. He ______________ (feel) the Spirit of the Mountain would be a good husband. So he ______________ (send) Mi Noung off to live with the Spirit of the Mountain.

Then the Spirit of the Sea ______________ (arrive) at the palace. When the Spirit of the Sea ______________ (see) that he ______________ (be) late, he ______________ (become) angry. He ______________ (start) a big storm. The wind ______________ (blow), the rain ______________ (fall), and the ocean ______________ (rise).

The battle between the Spirit of the Sea and the Spirit of the Mountain ______________ (continue) day and night. The Spirit of the Mountain ______________ (use) magic to make his mountain higher. He ______________ (take) Mi Noung to the very top.

At last the Spirit of the Sea ______________ (see) that he could not defeat the Spirit of the Mountain. The big storm ______________ (end). And Mi Noung ______________ (stay) with her husband on the high mountain near the sea.

Name ____________________

Who am I?

Characters
Princess Mi Noung
The Emperor
The Spirit of the Sea
The Spirit of the Mountain

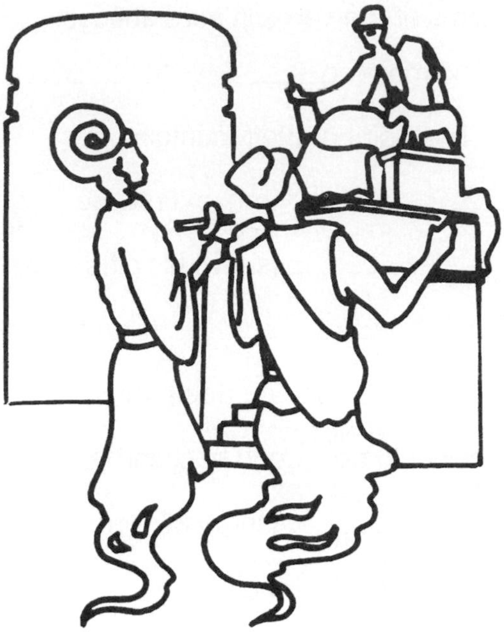

Read the descriptions of the characters in the story "Why the Monsoon Comes Each Year." Then write the name of each character by his or her description.

1. I brought the princess perfect pearls and tasty crabs.

   The Spirit of the Sea

2. I have only one daughter, so I want the best for her.

   ____

3. I married the princess and took her off to live in my home.

   ____

4. I finally let my daughter marry a powerful man. But there has been nothing but trouble since then.

   ____

5. I had many suitors, but my father did not like any of them.

   ____

6. I arrived too late and the princess had already married someone else.

   ____

7. I will never give up. I will keep fighting until the princess is my wife.

   ____

Name ____________________

Sound Search

Circle each word that contains the vowel sound as in the word *found.* Remember, this sound may be spelled *ou* or *ow.*

1. Air is all around the earth. It pushes down on you all the time.
2. Warm air doesn't push down very hard. An area with a warm air mass over it is called a low pressure area.
3. A front forms a boundary between two different air masses. Powerful storms may happen at fronts.
4. Water in the air forms clouds. Then the water falls to earth as rain or snow.
5. We know that rain is important to our survival. Some people hate to go outside when it rains. But they should remember that April showers bring May flowers.

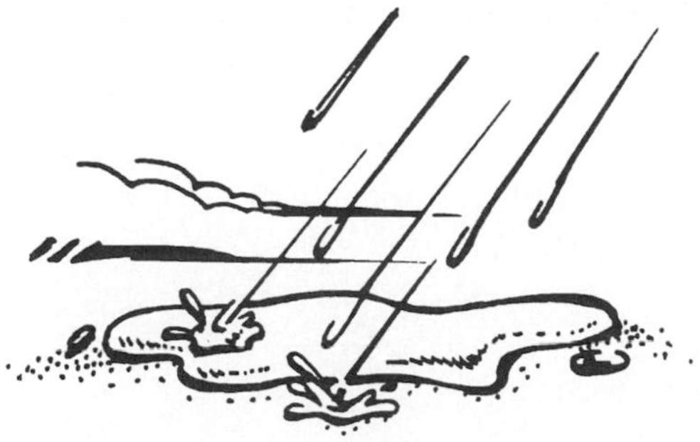

Name ____

Reading Objectives: Identify supporting ideas in a variety of written texts.

Summarize a variety of written texts.

Perceive relationships and recognize outcomes in a variety of written texts.

Clues

1. When you take tests, many of the questions will ask you to recall specific facts that support the main idea. These are important statements that give details about the topic.
2. Some questions will ask you to find the main idea or the best summary. The summary is the main idea but also includes important details.
3. Look for special clue words such as *because* and *since* to answer questions. These words signal cause-and-effect relationships. Reread to make sure you have the right answer.

Sample

Air is all around everything on Earth. It has different temperatures depending on where it is located. Large bodies of air, called air masses, move to make changes in the weather. This is what makes it hot in some places on Earth while it is cold in others.

Which of the following is the main idea of this passage?

A. Large bodies of air are masses.

B. Air masses of different temperatures move to make weather change.

C. Some places on Earth are hot while other places on Earth are cold.

D. Air is everywhere, and air masses move around a lot.

If you chose B, you are right. B is the only choice that tells both about air masses and about how air masses affect temperature and weather.

Name ______________________________

Try It

Read the passage carefully. Mark the circle next to the correct answer for each question.

The Monsoon

Once there was a princess who was sad because she was growing old and she was not married. Many men wanted to marry her, but none was great or powerful enough for her father, the Emperor.

One day, two strangers came to the Emperor's court. One was the Spirit of the Sea and the other was the Spirit of the Mountain. They were both rich, handsome, and powerful. How could the Emperor choose between them for his daughter? He gave them a challenge to see who could return first with gifts.

Early the next day, the Spirit of the Mountain arrived with jewels and fruit. The princess became his bride. As they were leaving the palace, the Spirit of the Sea came with his gifts. He was angry that he was late, and so he started a fight.

As the two spirits fought, the winds howled and waters whirled. There was a huge storm. Eventually, the Spirit of the Sea gave up and went back to the sea. However, each year he returns to do battle.

1. What is the best summary for this passage?

   ○ A princess did not have a husband because her father wanted a powerful one for her. Finally she had two suitors. Even though one won her fairly, the two suitors fought over her, causing a monsoon.

   ○ The Spirit of the Mountain and Spirit of the Sea fought over the princess. This caused a monsoon.

   ○ The princess was very worried because she was getting old. She thought she would never have a husband. She was worried.

   ○ The Emperor was a mean man who did not want his daughter to have a husband. He didn't think any one was rich or powerful enough. He issued a challenge to men who wanted to marry her.

2. According to the story, the monsoon comes every year because

   ○ the weather changes

   ○ the air masses change

   ○ the Spirit of the Sea is angry

   ○ a hurricane forms

Name ______________________

What should I wear?

Read the weather forecasts. Choose clothing to fit with the weather. Use the words in the box. Write your choices on the lines.

boots	hat	shorts	T-shirt
coat	jacket	sunglasses	umbrella
gloves	scarf	sweater	

1. The weather tomorrow will be sunny and hot.

______________ ______________ ______________

______________ ______________ ______________

2. The weather tomorrow will be snowy and cold.

______________ ______________ ______________

______________ ______________ ______________

3. Tomorrow will be rainy, windy, and cool.

______________ ______________ ______________

______________ ______________ ______________

4. Tomorrow will be breezy and cool. It might rain in the afternoon.

______________ ______________ ______________

______________ ______________ ______________

Name ____

What is it used for?

Match the weather tools with how meteorologists use them. Draw lines.

1. Meteorologists use an anemometer

2. Meteorologists use a thermometer

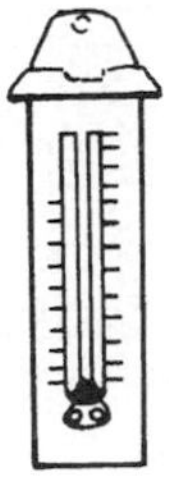

3. Meteorologists use a barometer

4. Meteorologists use a rain gauge

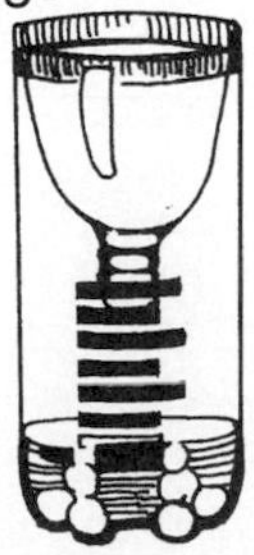

to measure air pressure.

to measure wind speed.

to measure rainfall.

to measure temperature.

Write sentences about why you use gloves, coats, boots, and umbrellas.

1. gloves I use gloves to keep my hands warm.
2. boots ____
3. coat ____
4. umbrella ____

Name ______________________________

What's the reason?

Complete the sentences. Use the choices in the box.

so they can protect their crops.
so they know when it is unsafe to fly and what the weather will be like in the air.
so they can wear the right clothes to keep them warm or cool.
so they know when to have snow plows ready.
so they can plan their construction work.
so they know when to cancel school.

1. People need to know about the weather

____

2. Airports need to know about winter storms

____

3. Farmers need to know about the weather

____

4. Builders need to know about the weather

____

5. Pilots need to know about the weather

____

6. Schools need to know about the weather

____

Name ______________________________

Wind Speed

Use this chart to complete the activity on pages 68 and 69 in the Student Book.

My Record	
Date	Wind Speed

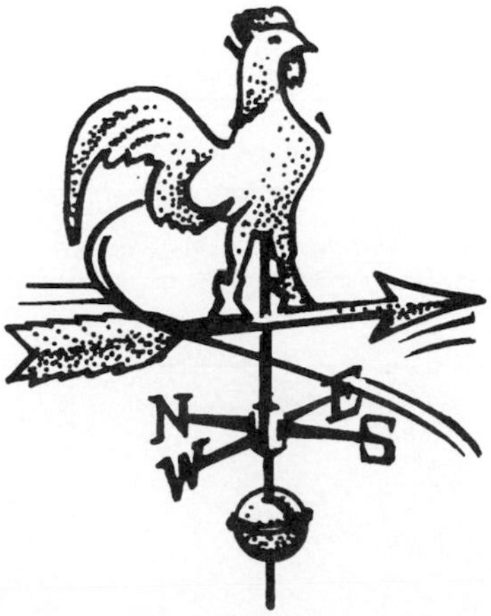

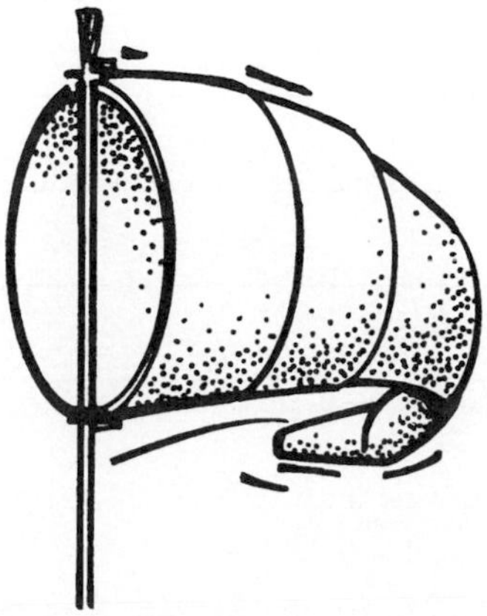

Name ______________________________

What's the weather going to be?

This is what the weather will be in four cities. Write a weather report for each city.

Chicago
cool
cloudy in the afternoon
rain at night

Juneau
cold
cloudy in the morning
snow in the afternoon.

New York
warm
rainy in the morning
cool in the afternoon

Miami
hot
sunny
windy

In Chicago, it is going to be cool.

____

____

In Juneau, ______________________________

____

____

In New York, ______________________________

____

____

In Miami ______________________________

____

____

Name ___

Weather Puzzle

Use these words to complete the puzzle.

BREEZY	CLEAR	OVERCAST	TEMPERATURE
CALM	CLOUDY	PRECIPITATION	WIND SPEED

What is the weather like today? Write about it. Use as many words from the puzzle as you can.

___

___

___

Name ____

Weather Patterns

Put weather words in the pictures of the sun, the cloud, and the raindrop to write your own concrete poem.

Ideas:

1. You might fill in the drop with different words about rain.
2. You might write words that tell about your favorite kind of weather.

Name ____________________

Long a Sound

The sound of long *a* can be spelled these ways:
say
rain
ate
they

Circle the words with long *a* sounds.

and
day
ask
make
rain
ran

way
pane
they
daily
math
state

Circle the words with long *a* sounds.

1. One way meteorologists study weather is to study the amount of rain. They also keep track of wind and air pressure.
2. Hail and rain are forms of water.
3. One place in the United States got 390 inches of snow in one month.
4. Many people listen to daily weather forecasts. It helps them know what kinds of clothes they will need for the next day.
5. People who want to be meteorologists take courses in math. They also study science.
6. Forty-three inches of rain fell in one day in a town in Texas in 1979.

Name ____________________

Science Objective: Demonstrate the ability to interpret scientific data and/or information.

Clues

1. When you take tests, some questions will ask you to interpret data about scientific models, organisms, events, or processes.
2. Other questions will ask you to give definitions of objects, organisms, actions, events, or processes. These will also include stating relationships.

Sample

People are very interested in the weather. You can see weather reporters on TV newscasts and hear them on the radio. Some reporters are also meteorologists. They have taken college courses in science and math. They have taken special courses on weather. They can use their knowledge to use special tools that measure the weather. They can use their knowledge to predict the weather.

A person who has special training in studying the weather is called

A. a weather reporter
B. a pilot
C. a newscaster
D. a meteorologist

This question asks for a definition. Use the information you learned to figure out the answer. The right choice is D, meteorologist. The others are people who may make statements about the weather, but they may not have had special training.

Name ______________________________

Try It

Read the questions. Mark the circle next to the correct answer for each question.

1. Which of the following tools is NOT used by a meteorologist to interpret data?
   - ○ barometer
   - ○ anemometer
   - ○ gasometer
   - ○ thermometer

2. What will happen when a barometer reading goes down?
   - ○ The sun will fade away.
   - ○ Clouds will turn very white.
   - ○ The weather will change.
   - ○ Measurement is completed.

Use the map to answer questions 3 and 4.

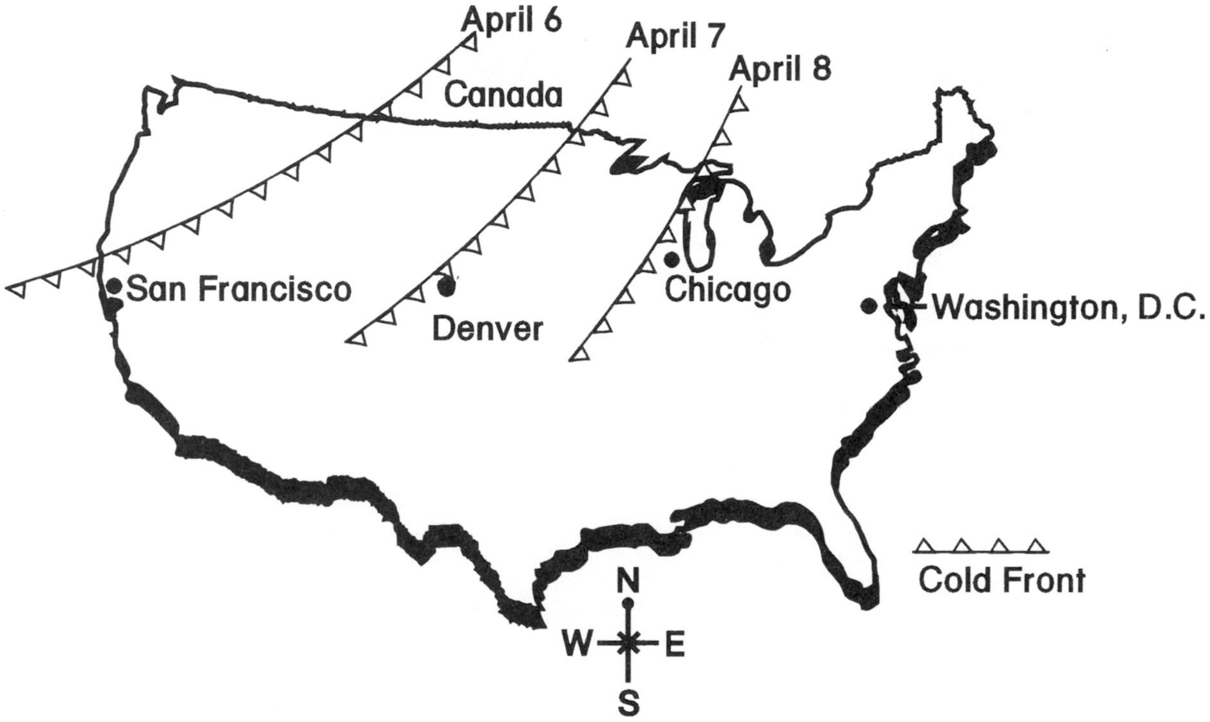

3. In which direction is the front moving?
   - ○ East
   - ○ Southwest
   - ○ North
   - ○ Northwest

4. Where will the front probably be on April 9?
   - ○ San Francisco
   - ○ Denver
   - ○ Chicago
   - ○ Washington, D.C.

Name ________________________________

What is it made of?

Use this page to write down what some of your clothes are made of. Look at the labels.

Word Bank

cotton
leather
nylon
polyester
wool

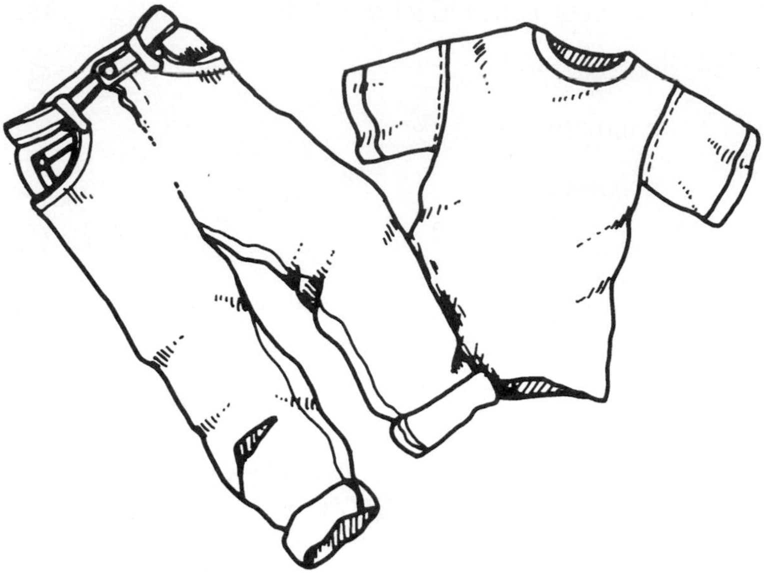

My Record		
Piece of Clothing	What It Is Made Of	Where It Was Made

Name ____

Supporting Details

Read the sentences below. Then circle the main idea sentence. Write the supporting details on the lines below.

Most slaves worked in farm fields, but some slaves did other jobs. Some slaves worked as servants in their owners' homes. Some slaves cooked the food. Some slaves cared for their owners' children. Some slaves built and repaired buildings from brick and wood. Some slaves made horse shoes. Slave owners often hired out these skilled slaves for wages. Some slaves earned enough money to buy their own freedom.

____

____

____

____

____

____

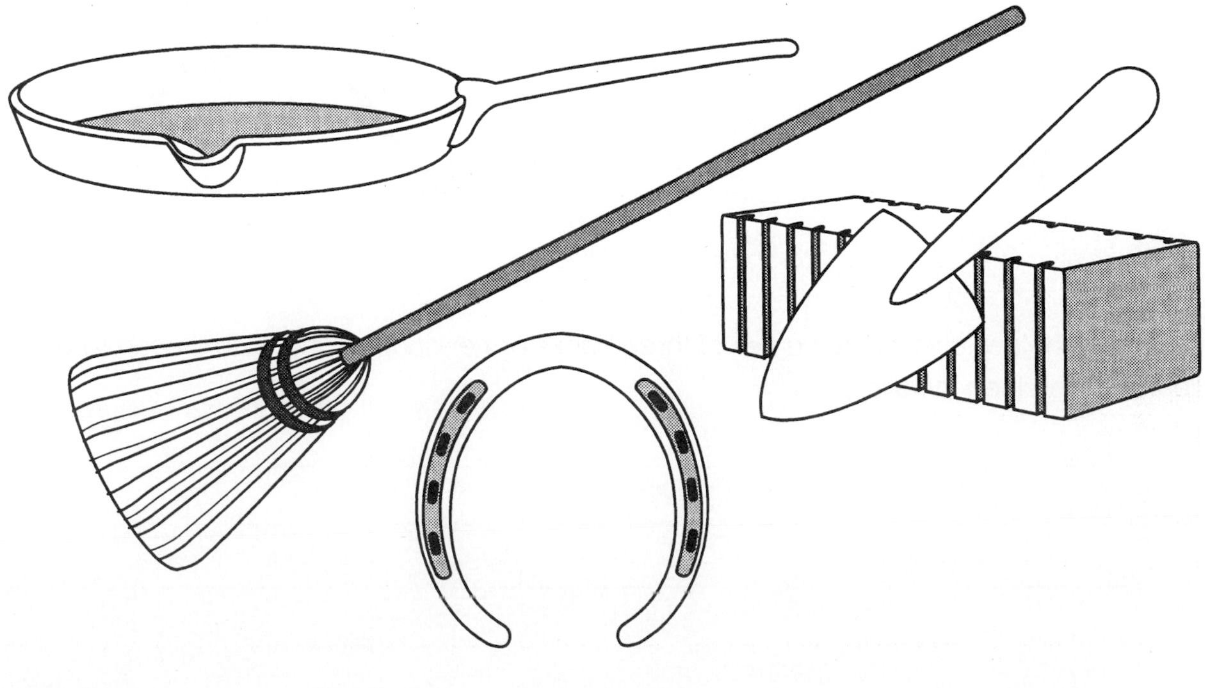

Name ______________________________

Using Italics

Read the sentences. Circle the names that should be in italics.

Many people have written books about the Civil War. One of these books is Gone with the Wind. It was written by Margaret Mitchell, who lived in Atlanta, Georgia. The book talks about a woman named Scarlett O'Hara, her family, and a man named Rhett Butler. In the story, Scarlett's father owns a large plantation called Tara. After the Civil War, Scarlett tries to make Tara a great plantation again. In 1939, Gone With the Wind was made into a movie starring Vivien Leigh and Clark Gable. Both the book and movie versions of Gone with the Wind were very popular.

Another book about the Civil War was written by Stephen Crane. The book is called The Red Badge of Courage. It talks about a young northern soldier named Henry Fleming. The Red Badge of Courage is often read by students in Grade 8.

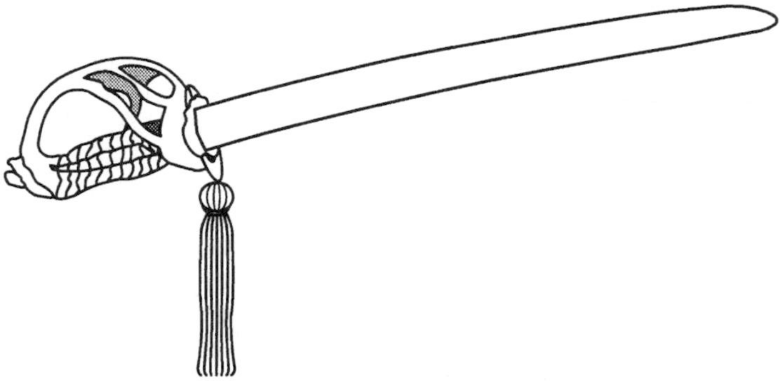

Use the lines below to write the names of three books or newspapers that would need to be underlined or written in italics.

____

____

____

Name ______________________________

Reading Graphs

Study the graph and answer the questions.

Bushels of Wheat and Corn Grown on the Gordon Family Farm, 1831–1835

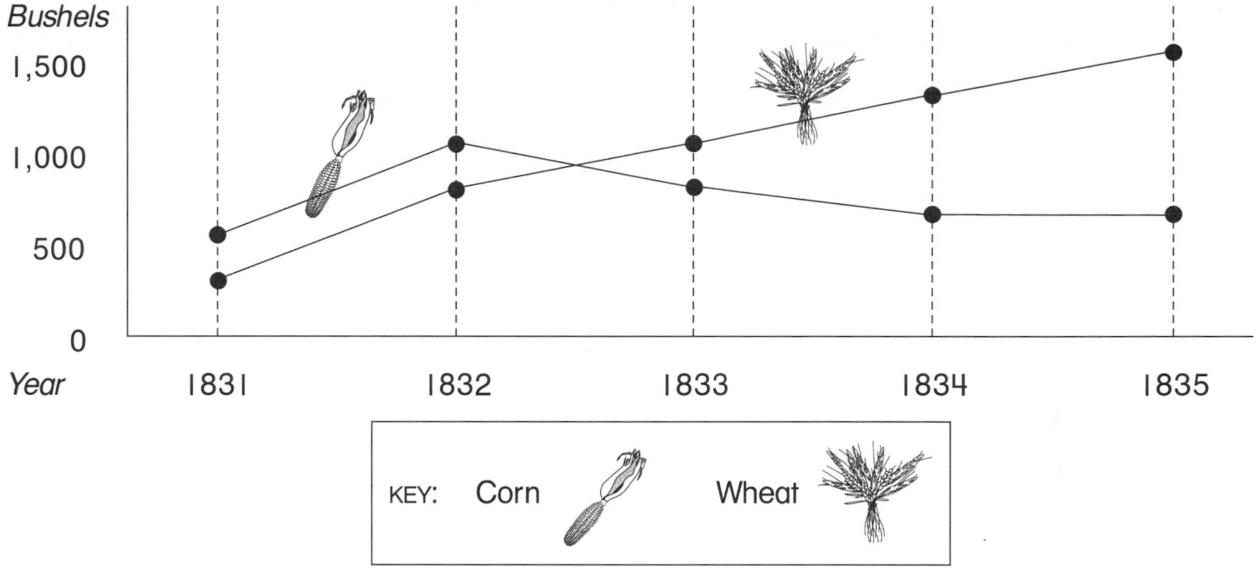

1. In what year did the Gordon family grow the most corn? ______________________

2. About how many bushels of wheat did the Gordon family grow in 1833? ______________________

____

3. In what year did the Gordon family grow about 250 bushels of wheat? ______________________

4. About how many bushels of wheat and corn together did the Gordon family grow in 1834?

____

5. In what year did the farm produce the most crops? ______________________

Name ____

Important People and Places

Use the clues to complete the crossword puzzle.

Across

2. woman who wrote *Uncle Tom's Cabin*
5. man who started *The Liberator*
6. woman who was the Underground Railroad's most famous conductor

Down

1. man who started *The North Star*
3. southern sisters who freed their own family's slaves
4. the part of the United States where most slaves lived

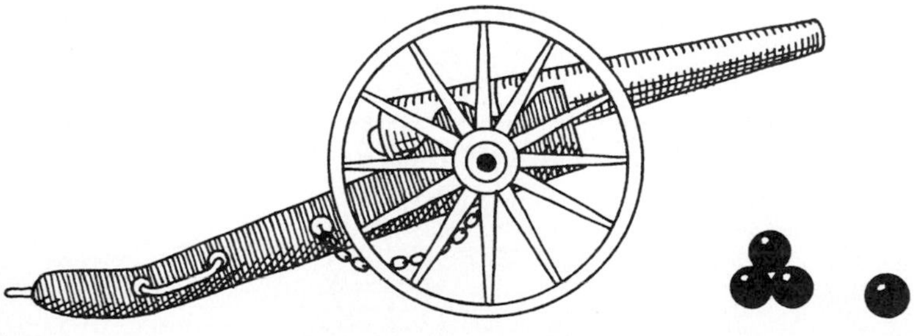

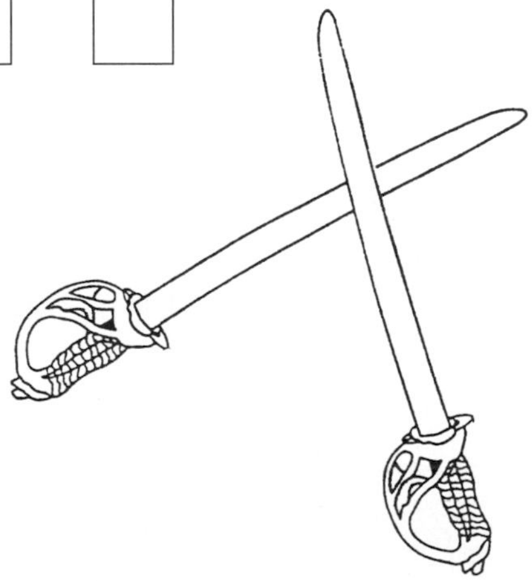

Name ______________________________

Writing About the Past

Write the correct form of the words to talk about things that happened in the past.

Most slaves ________________ (live) in the South. They ________________ (work) in farm fields. Some slaves ________________ (escape). They ________________ (travel) north at night in secret. During the day, they ________________ (hide). Slaves who got caught ________________ (return) to the South. Usually their owners ________________ (punish) them.

Harriet Tubman was an escaped slave. She ________________ (lead) many escaping slaves to safety on the Underground Railroad. She ________________ (return) to the South many times. She ________________ (help) hundreds of people escape.

Frederick Douglass was an escaped slave. He ________________ (oppose) slavery. He ________________ (start) a newspaper he ________________ (call) *The North Star.* He ________________ (become) a strong leader of the abolitionist cause.

Name ____

Vocabulary Review

Circle these words in the puzzle.

Canals
Factories
Rights
Civil War
North

Slavery
Plantation
South
Conductor
Underground Railroad

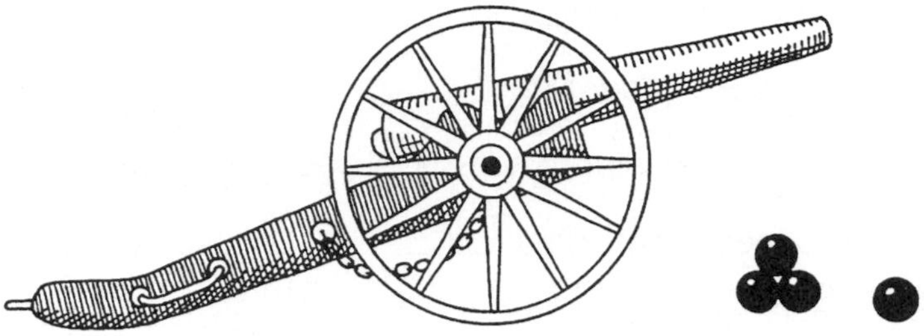

A	Y	V	K	L	W	S	L	A	V	E	R	Y	K	F	C	F	A	I
W	P	C	I	V	I	L	W	A	R	C	O	N	D	U	C	T	O	R
S	L	J	K	E	Z	X	W	U	P	L	A	N	T	A	T	I	O	N
R	I	G	H	T	S	S	A	L	X	R	X	A	V	Z	Q	V	C	Y
U	N	D	E	R	G	R	O	U	N	D	R	A	I	L	R	O	A	D
Z	H	O	O	O	J	M	J	U	W	H	P	E	Q	B	T	O	N	B
T	F	L	R	P	K	L	S	F	T	J	B	E	R	B	V	K	A	P
Q	W	R	X	T	M	I	Q	A	B	H	K	V	L	T	C	N	L	T
T	U	H	O	V	H	X	J	F	A	C	T	O	R	I	E	S	S	V

Name ______________________________

Using Contractions

Circle the correct contraction in each sentence.

I'm/I've a student in this school. This year I'm/I've in Grade 8. Next year, I'm/I've going to be in Grade 9. Sometimes, I'm/I've got a lot of homework. Most of the students I'm/I've talked to think there should be no homework on the weekends, but I study a lot on the weekends. Sometimes, I'm/I've got to study hard to keep up with the class. But I'm/I've working hard to learn English.

Write about yourself. What grade are you in? How are you doing in school? Use the contractions *I'm* and *I've.*

____

____

____

____

____

____

____

Name ____

Writing Objectives: Respond appropriately in a written composition to the purpose/audience specified in a given topic.

Organize ideas in a written composition on a given topic.

Demonstrate control of the English language in a written composition on a given topic.

Generate a written composition that develops/supports/elaborates the central idea stated in a given topic.

Clues

1. These objectives should be worked on over a period of time until you are sure you know the difference between the required compositions.
2. When you take tests, you will be given one of the following prompts:

Prompt	Sample Topic
Describe an object, person, place, situation, or picture. ➡	Write a composition to describe a special school activity.
Write a composition to tell how to do something. ➡	Write directions to tell your friend how to make super nachos. Make sure you include all the steps.
Write a composition to classify ideas, objects, or people according to criteria given. ➡	Write both good things and bad things about having to ride the bus to school.
Formulate a position on a given issue to convince an audience. ➡	Your principal is thinking about adding a taco stand to the cafeteria. The stand would be from a fast-food chain. What is your position? Convince your principal to see your point of view.

Name ______________________________

Try It

Use your own paper to write a composition. Choose one of the prompts from page 50. Write about the sample topic given for the prompt or choose your own topic.

Here is some information about how your writing will be scored on tests.

1. Some errors in language mechanics, sentence structure, and usage may occur. You are not penalized for these unless they are so frequent that they make it difficult for the reader to understand your response.
2. Your score will not be affected by spelling unless numerous errors in basic, familiar words occur so that it is hard for the reader to follow your meaning.
3. Your score will not be affected by inaccurate punctuation.
4. Your score will be lowered for the following:

   A. Use of the improper mode for the given writing prompt

   B. Composition too brief

   C. Responses that drift from the topic

   D. Responses that have gaps

   E. Responses that do not communicate ideas

Name ______________________________

Causes of the Civil War

Put the correct number from Column B in the blank in Column A to make true sentences.

Column A	Column B
The North had ____	1. many large farms.
In the South, there were ____	2. slavery was needed.
Slavery was legal in ____	3. elected President of the United States.
Abolitionists believed ____	4. the South.
Many southern plantation owners believed ____	5. many railroads and factories.
Abraham Lincoln was ____	6. seceded from the United States.
Some southern states ____	7. slavery was bad.

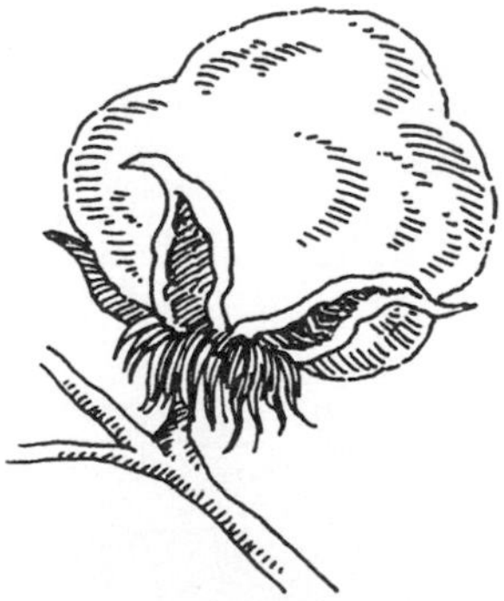

Name ______________________________

Using Commas

Read the sentences. Add commas to the numbers that need them.

In 1860, Abraham Lincoln was elected President of the United States. He got 1 8 6 5 9 0 8 votes. His main opponent, Stephen A. Douglas, got 1 3 8 0 2 0 2 votes. Other people got 1 4 3 8 9 2 0 votes.

At the start of the war, Lincoln called for 7 5 0 0 0 soldiers to serve for 90 days. The South called for 1 0 0 0 0 0 men to serve for 12 months. In all, about 8 0 0 0 0 0 men served in the South's armies. About 2 1 0 0 0 0 0 men served in the North's armies.

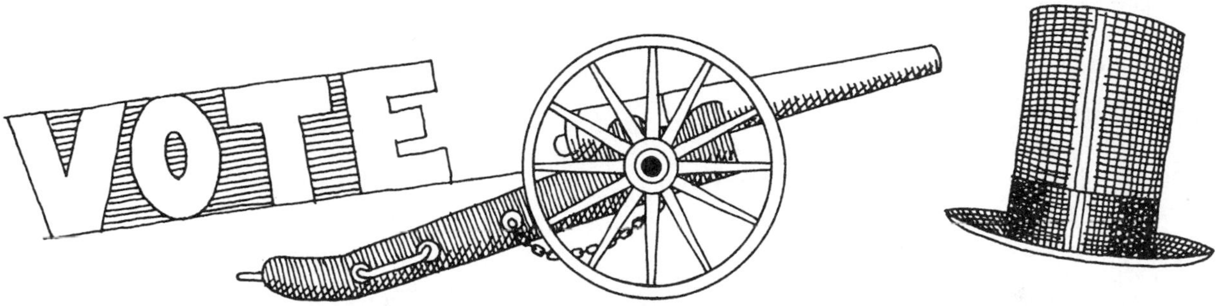

Use the lines below to write three numbers that do need commas and three numbers that do not.

____

____

____

Name ____

Stating Opinions

Choose a word from the group below to complete each sentence. More than one choice may be correct.

believed	respected	thought	trusted

When the Civil War began, many people ______________ it would not last long. They ______________ that not many soldiers would be hurt or killed. They ______________ that the war would be over in a few weeks. People in both the North and the South ______________ this. Within a few months, people on both sides ______________ differently.

People in the North ______________ Abe Lincoln. They ______________ that he would do a good job as President. They ______________ that he could help win the war for the North. People in the South ______________ that Robert E. Lee was such a good general that they would win easily. They ______________ him as a person and as a soldier.

Use the lines below to write a sentence using one of these four words: *believe, respect, think, trust*. Give your ideas about Civil War events and people.

____

____

____

____

Name ____________________

Abe Lincoln

Number the facts about Abe Lincoln so they are in the order in which these things happened to him.

_____ His mother died when Abe was 9 years old.

_____ In the 1840s, Abe Lincoln married Mary Todd.

_____ In 1864, Abe Lincoln was reelected President of the United States.

_____ Abe Lincoln was born in a log cabin in 1809.

_____ In 1830, the Lincoln family moved to Illinois.

_____ Six months later, Abe Lincoln was shot and killed as he watched a play.

_____ Abe Lincoln became President in 1861, and the family moved to Washington, D. C.

Name ______________________________

Using *-er* and *-ist* Words

Add the correct word from the list to each of the sentences.

abolitionist
conductor
founder
leader
novelist
photographer
owner
soldier

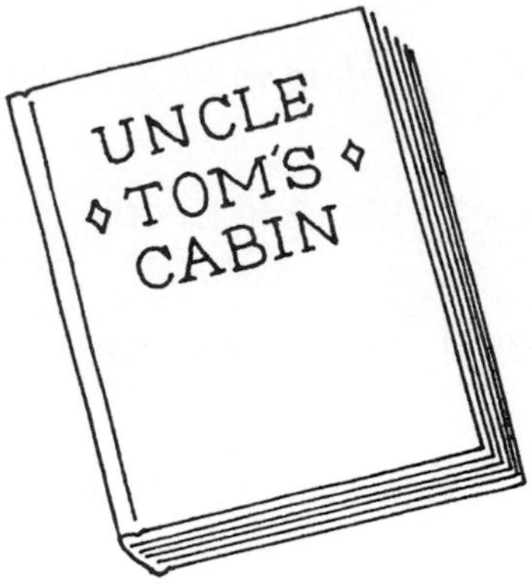

1. Mathew Brady was a ______________ who took many pictures of the Civil War.

2. Harriet Tubman was the most famous ______________ on the Underground Railroad.

3. Clara Barton was the ______________ of the American Red Cross.

4. Robert E. Lee was a ______________ before the Civil War.

5. Frederick Douglass was an ______________ and started a newspaper called *The North Star.*

6. Abe Lincoln was the ______________ of the North during the Civil War.

7. Harriet Beecher Stowe was a ______________ who wrote *Uncle Tom's Cabin.*

Name ________________________________

Civil War People

Choose two people you have learned about in this unit. Complete the charts about them.

Name of Person
What I Learned About the Person
What I Would Like to Learn About the Person
What I Would Like to Ask the Person
Why I Am Interested in the Person

Name of Person
What I Learned About the Person
What I Would Still Like to Learn About the Person
What I Would Like to Ask the Person
Why I Am Interested in the Person

Name ______________________________

Vocabulary

Use the clues to do the crossword puzzle.

Across

2. escaped slave who started *The North Star*
4. part of the United States that was mostly farms
7. man who led the North during the Civil War
8. man who started *The Liberator*
10. what the United States was involved in from 1861 to 1865
11. woman who wrote *Uncle Tom's Cabin*

Down

1. part of the United States where most of the railroads and factories were
3. someone who opposed slavery
5. what connected Lake Erie to the Hudson River
6. how most African Americans in the South lived
9. name of the man who led the South's armies

Name ______________________________

Thunder at Gettysburg

Tillie did many things in the story *Thunder at Gettysburg.* Number the events in the order they happened in the story.

_____Tillie left the Weikerts' farm in a wagon when officers told people to go to a safe place.

_____Early in the morning Tillie went to take tea to the wounded soldier she had met the night before.

_____Tillie stopped at a gray farmhouse that was crowded with people.

_____Tillie learned that General Weed, the wounded solider, was dead.

_____Tillie started to help by carrying water and making bandages.

_____Tillie sat on the grass and thought about what had happened in the battle and what war meant.

_____Tillie learned that the North had won the battle.

_____There was a sudden silence.

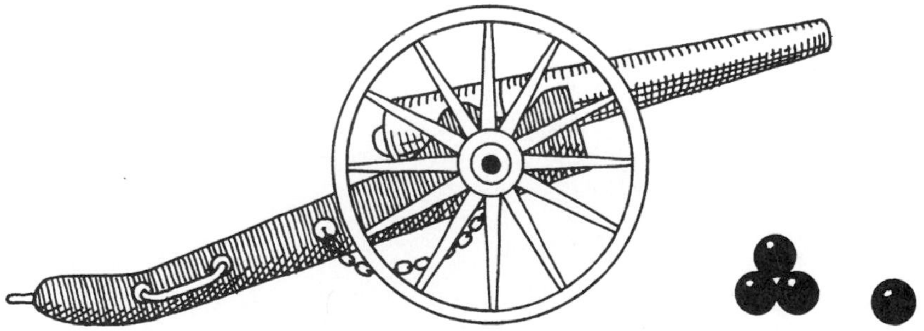

Write what you thought of this story. It is based on the true story of a young girl who lived in Gettysburg.

____

____

____

____

____

____

Name ______________________________

Social Studies Objective: Demonstrate an understanding of historical concepts and information.

Clues

1. When you take tests, some questions will ask you to recall and analyze the contributions of significant individuals in the history of your state, the United States, and the world. Some questions may ask you to analyze major events in history.
2. Other questions will ask you to identify major world civilizations of the past and their contributions to the present.

Samples

1. During which decade was the U.S. Civil War fought?

   A. The 1940s

   B. The 1860s

   C. The 1780s

   D. The 1890s

   B is the correct answer. The Civil War lasted from 1861 to 1865.

2. When the Civil War began, most people in the South were

   A. sailors

   B. farmers

   C. immigrants

   D. factory workers

   The correct answer is B. Most people in the South still made their livings as farmers.

Name ____________________

Try It

Read each question. Mark the circle next to the correct answer for each question.

1. Harriet Tubman became famous for her work
   - ○ as a public speaker for women's rights
   - ○ on the Underground Railroad
   - ○ as a newspaper publisher
   - ○ on the development of new foods

2. The Civil War was fought because the nation was divided about
   - ○ breaking away from Great Britain
   - ○ the Industrial Revolution
   - ○ slavery and states' rights
   - ○ freedom of the press

3. Abraham Lincoln and Robert E. Lee were both
   - ○ army generals
   - ○ from Illinois
   - ○ supporters of states' rights
   - ○ leaders during the Civil War

4. An abolitionist was someone who
   - ○ opposed slavery
   - ○ supported the South during the Civil War
   - ○ worked in a factory
   - ○ supported slavery

Name ______________________________

Space Word Search

Complete the words in the sentences.
Then find each completed word in the puzzle.

1. P ___ ___ ___ ___ ___ s orbit the S ___ n.

2. M ___ ___ ___ s orbit the planets.

3. The Sun is a s ___ ___ r.

4. The u ___ ___ ___ ___ ___ ___ e contains all stars and all space.

5. C ___ ___ ___ ___ s are made of rock and ice.

6. A ___ ___ ___ ___ ___ ___ ___ s are pieces of rock and metal that orbit the Sun.

A	S	O	M	X	R	F	Z	M	H	E	T	I	A	K
D	U	C	E	W	S	Y	U	N	I	V	E	R	S	E
R	N	B	O	E	E	C	A	E	F	P	H	L	T	P
P	L	A	N	E	T	S	G	C	E	S	S	I	E	J
M	Y	T	V	O	I	Z	N	T	O	L	O	A	R	G
S	O	L	S	T	U	E	R	P	Q	M	D	N	O	D
K	X	O	S	J	T	V	Q	N	J	T	E	S	I	S
A	S	M	N	U	R	U	U	R	E	I	M	T	D	S
C	W	N	V	S	T	A	R	Z	S	C	N	C	S	B

Name ______________________________

Where are they?

Complete the sentences with the words in the box. Use the information on pages 118 and 119 in the Student Book.

Word Bank	
around	from
between	next to
close to	to
far from	

1. Comets are balls of rock and ice. They orbit the Sun. Their orbit takes them ____________ the Sun and then ____________ the Sun. When comets are ____________ the Sun, they form tails.
2. The planet Mercury is ____________ the Sun. It is also ____________ Earth.
3. The planet Venus is also ____________ the Sun. It is ____________ Earth.
4. The Moon travels ____________ Earth.
5. Light travels ____________ the Sun ____________ the planets in the solar system.
6. Planets that are ____________ the Sun are colder. Planets that are ____________ the Sun are hotter.
7. There are many asteroids ____________ Jupiter and Mars.
8. The planet Uranus is ____________ Saturn and Neptune.
9. The Moon orbits Earth. It is ____________ Earth, and it travels ____________ Earth.
10. Comets, asteroids, and planets travel ____________ the Sun.
11. Thirty trips ____________ Earth are equal to one trip ____________ the Moon.
12. The planet Pluto is ____________ Earth.

Name ______________________________

Solar System Facts

True or False? Write *T* or *F* in the blanks.

If a sentence is false, write a correct sentence on the lines.
Use the information on pages 120 and 121 of the Student Book.

1. __F__ The Sun is a planet, like Earth or Mars.

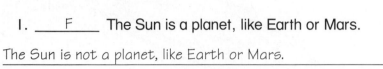

The Sun is not a planet, like Earth or Mars.

2. ________ Most of the light and heat from the Sun gets to Earth.

3. ________ The planets close to the Sun are very hot, and the planets far away from the Sun are very cold.

4. ________ The Sun is made of solid rock and metal.

5. ________ The Sun is a star that is much different from other stars in the universe.

6. ________ The core of the Sun is cooler than the outside of the Sun.

7. ________ The Sun is a yellow dwarf. That means it is not in the hottest group of stars.

Name ______________________________

The Metric System

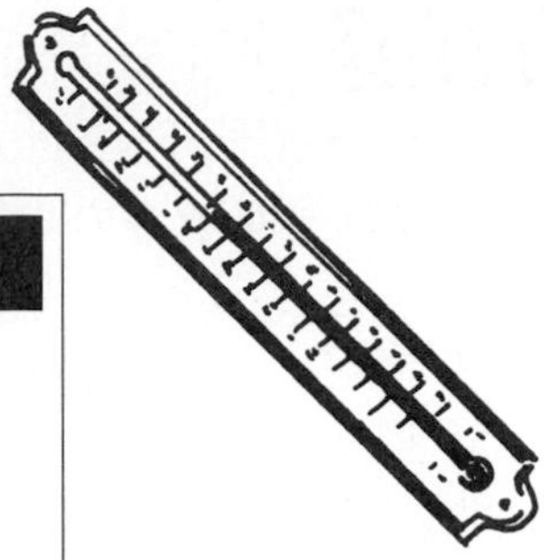

Word Bank

Kilometers = Miles x 1.6
Miles = Kilometers x .6

Celsius degrees = (Fahrenheit degrees - 32)/1.8
Fahrenheit degrees = (Celsius degrees x 1.8) + 32

Solve the problems. Convert to the unit of measurement in parentheses. Use the information in the box. Show how you found each answer.

1. 180 miles (kilometers)

180 miles x 1.6 = 288 kilometers

2. 68 kilometers (miles)

____

3. 98.6 degrees Fahrenheit (degrees Celsius)

____

4. 38 degrees Celsius (degrees Fahrenheit)

____

Answer the questions. Show how you found the answers.

1. Winds on Neptune can be 700 miles per hour. How many kilometers per hour is this?

____

2. The largest asteroid is about 970 kilometers in diameter. How many miles is this?

____

3. Mercury is a hot planet. But the side of Mercury away from the Sun can have temperatures as low as -279 degrees Fahrenheit. How many degrees Celsius is this?

____

4. The highest temperature recorded on Earth was 58 degrees Celsius. How many degrees Fahrenheit is this?

____

Name ____________________

Few or *Little*?

Complete the sentences about space and the solar system. Use the words *few* or *little.*

1. There are very __________ things in space.
2. __________ heat from the Sun reaches Earth.
3. __________ planets in the solar system have rings around them.
4. In space, there are __________ things to reflect light.
5. It takes __________ time for a space ship to leave Earth's atmosphere.
6. Only a __________ meteors reach the Earth's surface.
7. We have very __________ information about planets outside of our solar system.
8. __________ people have walked on the Moon.
9. We have only a __________ understanding of how vast the universe is.
10. It takes sunlight only a __________ time to reach Earth.

Name ______________________________

Names of Nationalities

The Lincoln School did a survey of students who were born in countries other than the United States. Here are the results.

Country	Number of Students	Country	Number of Students
Brazil	2	Ukraine	5
Egypt	2	Mexico	4
China	2	Italy	1
Japan	6	India	2
Greece	1	Colombia	3
Korea	4		

Write sentences that tell the results of the survey. Do not start a new line for each sentence. Use the answers given as a model.

There are 2 Brazilian students. There are 2 Egyptian students. There are

How many students are there from each continent? Write sentences.

There are 4 North American students.

Name ______________________________

Name the planets.

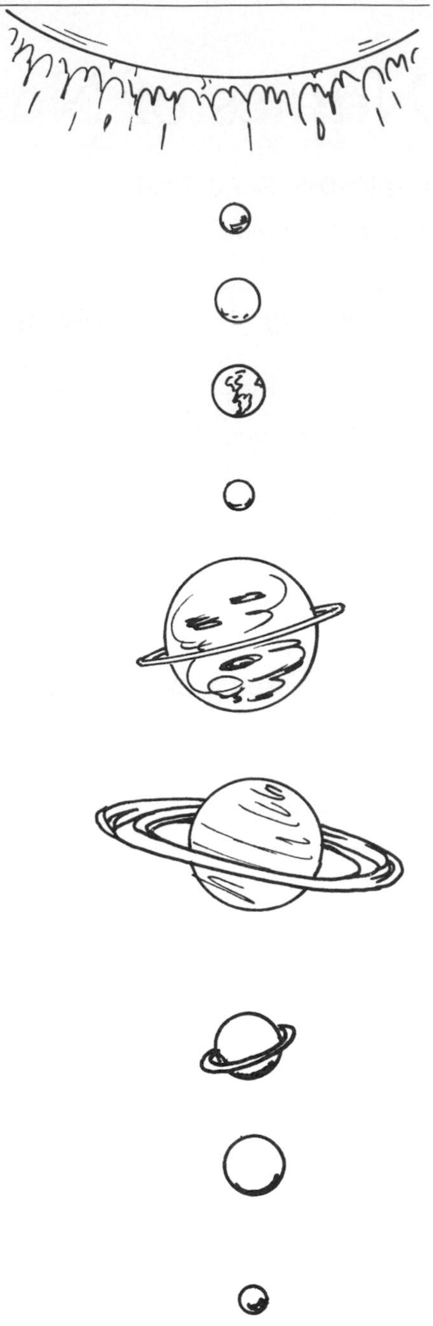

Use the clues to name the planets in the solar system.

1. This planet is farthest from the Sun.
   Its name has five letters.

   ____

2. This planet is closer to the Sun than Earth is.
   Its name begins with *v.*

   ____

3. This planet orbits the Sun faster than any other planet.
   Its name ends with *y.*

   ____

4. This planet is closer to the Sun than Jupiter.
   It has the shortest name of all the planets.

   ____

5. This planet orbits the Sun every 365 days.

   ____

6. This planet is the second farthest from the Sun.
   It is the only planet with two *e*'s in its name.

   ____

7. This planet is farther from the Sun than Mars is.
   The second letter in its name is *u.*

   ____

8. This planet is third farthest from the Sun.
   You can spell *sun* with the last three letters of its name.

   ____

9. This planet is between Jupiter and Uranus.
   Its name has six letters.

   ____

Name ______________________________

Homonyms

Circle the correct homonym to complete each sentence.

1. The (Son / Sun) is the center of the solar system.
   My father is my grandfather's (son / sun).
2. That is the (right / write) answer to the math problem.
   Mark is learning to read and (right / write) in English.

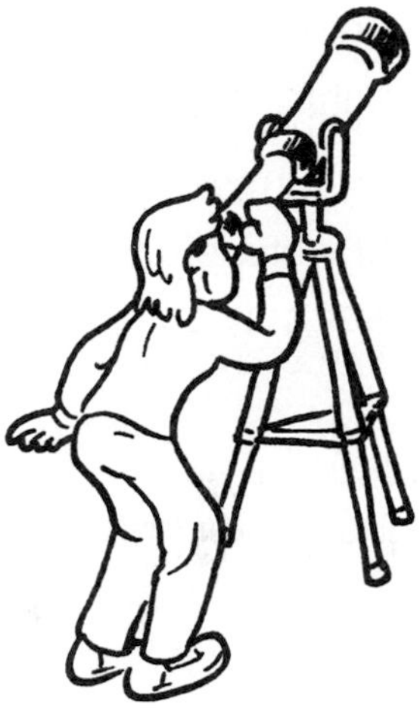

3. I would like to (hear / here) that song again.
   (Hear / Here) she comes!
4. You can (sea / see) the moon at night from Earth.
   Sonia likes to swim in the (sea / see).
5. Adam is studying to (be / bee) an astronomer.
   I yelled when the (be / bee) stung my arm.
6. Earth has only (one / won) moon.
   Lucinda (one / won) the bicycle race.
7. It looks as if someone (ate / eight) a part of the moon.
   When I was (ate / eight) years old, I lived in another country.
8. Did someone eat a (piece / peace) of the moon?
   People want (piece / peace) on Earth. They want all wars to stop.
9. The (main / mane) parts of the Sun are the core, photosphere, and chromosphere.
   The (main / mane) of a horse is the hair on its head.
10. The sun is a yellow star, not a (read / red) one.
    The class (read / red) an article about the solar system.
11. In the experiment, we cut a (whole / hole) in a box.
    The (whole / hole) world could easily fit inside the Sun or the planet Jupiter.
12. The volcano (threw / through) out rock and gases.
    In the experiment, we looked (threw / through) the top of the box.

Name ____

Math Objectives: Demonstrate an understanding of number concepts.
Estimate solutions to a problem situation.

Clues

1. When comparing and ordering fractions, draw fraction bars.

Example: $\frac{3}{4}$ 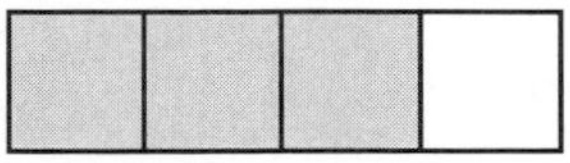

2. To estimate, round first and then solve. When you take tests, answer choices might include a range, so adjusting your answer may be appropriate.

Samples

1. Venus is the closest planet to Earth. It is 25,700,000 miles inside Earth's orbit. What is this distance in scientific notation?

   A. 257×10^5

   B. 2.57×10^5

   C. 2.57×10^4

   D. 2.57×10^7

Scientific notation is a convenient way to write large numbers. The number is written as a multiplication problem. The first number is from 1 to 10, and the second number is a power of 10.

$25{,}700{,}000 = 2.57 \times 10^7$.

The correct answer is D.

2. Mrs. Grabowski must take a typing test for a job interview. If she can type 62 words per minute, what is a good estimate of the number of words she can type in 5 minutes?

   A. 12

   B. 13

   C. 200

   D. 250

   E. 300

Round the number 62 to 60. Then multiply by 5.
$60 \times 5 = 300$.
The correct answer is E.

Name ______________________________

Try It

Read each question carefully. Mark the circle next to the correct answer.

1. Mercury's time of revolution around the sun is 87.9686 days. What is this number rounded to the nearest hundredths?

   - ○ 87.95
   - ○ 88
   - ○ 87.979
   - ○ 87.97

2. After Mr. Jenkins graded the science test, he figured out that 2/5 of the class made an A on the test. What percent of the class made an A on the test?

   - ○ 0.4%
   - ○ 20%
   - ○ 25%
   - ○ 40%

3. Omar has 71 pieces of gum to share among himself and 4 friends. What is a good estimate of the number of pieces of gum that each of the 5 people will receive?

   - ○ 12
   - ○ 14
   - ○ 17
   - ○ 18
   - ○ 20

4. Pierre made a long-distance call to his best friend, who lives in Paris, France. The first minute cost $1.45 and every additional minute cost $0.18. The total charge of the 6-minute phone call was between

   - ○ $1.00 and $2.00
   - ○ $2.00 and $3.00
   - ○ $3.00 and $4.00
   - ○ $4.00 and $5.00
   - ○ $5.00 and $6.00

Name ____________________

The Solar System

Draw a line from the words on the left to their definitions on the right.

1. asteroids	move around the Sun
2. atmosphere	gases that surround a planet
3. comets	Nine of these orbit the Sun.
4. gas	pieces of rock and metal that orbit the Sun
5. moons	the outside of a planet
6. orbit	Earth's air is an example.
7. planets	balls of rock and ice
8. rotate	They orbit planets.
9. Sun	turn around (causing day and night on planets)
10. surface	the center of the solar system

Find the words listed above in the puzzle. Circle them.

A	S	T	E	R	O	I	D	S	B	P	H	S	M	S	M	O	B	N
I	D	E	C	O	I	T	E	F	S	R	T	F	R	O	R	B	I	T
D	R	O	A	T	M	O	S	P	H	E	R	E	E	E	O	R	O	O
T	I	P	B	A	T	A	G	O	U	A	T	M	N	S	U	N	I	H
C	O	M	E	T	S	E	A	A	S	L	E	E	A	K	R	I	S	J
P	L	A	N	E	T	S	C	L	S	U	R	F	A	C	E	H	G	G

Name ______________________________

Comparing the Planets

Use comparatives to complete the sentences about the planets.
Use the chart on Student Book pages 134 and 135 to find the right answers.
Hint: One orbit of the Sun is one year. One rotation of a planet is one day.

1. Mercury is ____smaller____ than Earth. (size)
2. Neptune is ______________ from the Sun than Saturn is. (distance)
3. A day on Uranus is ______________ than a day on Saturn. (length)
4. Earth is ______________ than Mars. (temperature)
5. Uranus is ______________ than Venus. (size)
6. Jupiter is ______________ to the Sun than Neptune. (distance)
7. A year on Mercury is ______________ than a year on Venus. (length)
8. Pluto is ______________ than Mercury. (temperature)
9. Saturn is ______________ than Pluto. (temperature)
10. A year on Pluto is ______________ than a year on Uranus. (length)
11. Mars is ______________ to the Sun than Jupiter. (distance)
12. A day on Earth is ______________ than a day on Neptune. (length)
13. A year on Jupiter is ______________ than a year on Venus. (length)
14. Venus is ______________ than Jupiter. (size)
15. A day on Venus is ______________ than a day on Mars. (length)

Make your own comparisons between planets. Which do you find the most interesting?

____

____

____

____

____

____

____

Name ______________________________

Read and take notes.

Read the article about Mercury. Then fill in the missing notes.

Mercury

Mercury is the closest planet to the Sun. It is only a little larger than the Earth's moon. The planet was named after the Roman god Mercury. He was the swift messenger for the gods.

Because it is so near the Sun, Mercury can be very hot. The average temperature during the day is 662 degrees Fahrenheit (350 degrees Celsius). The only planet that gets hotter is Venus. Mercury can also be very, very cold. Temperatures on the side of the planet away from the Sun can be as low as -279 degrees Fahrenheit (-173 degrees Celsius).

Mercury orbits the Sun quickly. A year on Mercury lasts only 88 Earth days. However, Mercury rotates much more slowly than Earth. A day on Mercury lasts 59 Earth days. So a Mercury day is almost as long as a Mercury year.

Mercury has a rocky surface covered by craters. Small comets might have hit the planet and made the craters. Mercury has a metal core. It has no water and very little air. Unlike Earth, Mercury has no moon.

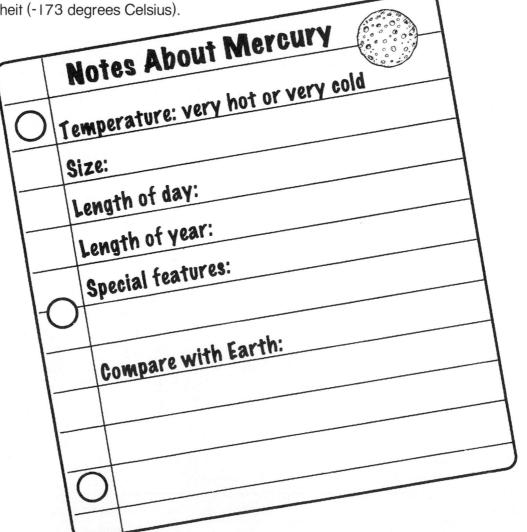

Notes About Mercury

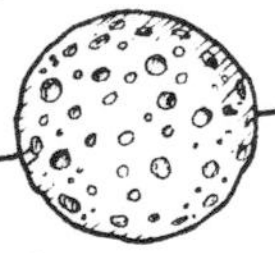

Temperature: very hot or very cold

Size:

Length of day:

Length of year:

Special features:

Compare with Earth:

Name ______________________________

An Imaginary Trip

Pretend that you are taking a trip to three other planets in the solar system, such as Mercury, Mars, and Jupiter. What would you see? To write about your imaginary trip, use your notes on Mercury from page 74 of this book. Also use the information in the Student Book.
Be sure to write about how the planets you see are the same and how they are different.

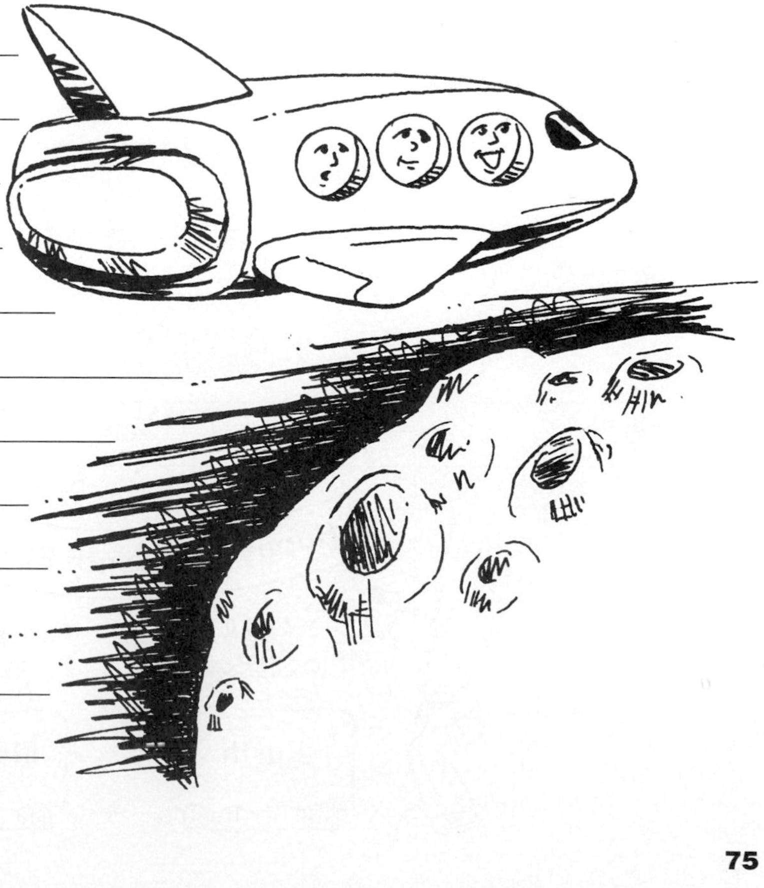

Name ____________________

If you lived on Mars, . . .

The charts show how much you would weigh and how old you would be if you lived on other planets.

Weight on Earth = 100 pounds	
Mercury	39 pounds
Venus	88 pounds
Mars	38 pounds
Jupiter	253 pounds
Saturn	107 pounds

Age on Earth = 13	
Mercury	54 years old
Venus	21 years old
Mars	7 years old
Jupiter	13 months old
Saturn	5 months old

Use the chart. Write three pairs of sentences like the examples below.

Example:

If you weighed 100 pounds on Earth, you would weigh 107 pounds on Saturn.

If you were 13 years old on Earth, you would be 5 months old on Saturn.

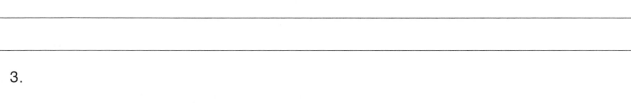

1. ____________________

____

2. ____________________

____

3. ____________________

____

Name ______________________________

Facts About the Solar System

Look at the articles about the solar system on pages 140 to 151 in the Student Book. Pick out one or two facts that you think are interesting about each thing listed below. Write sentences with those facts.

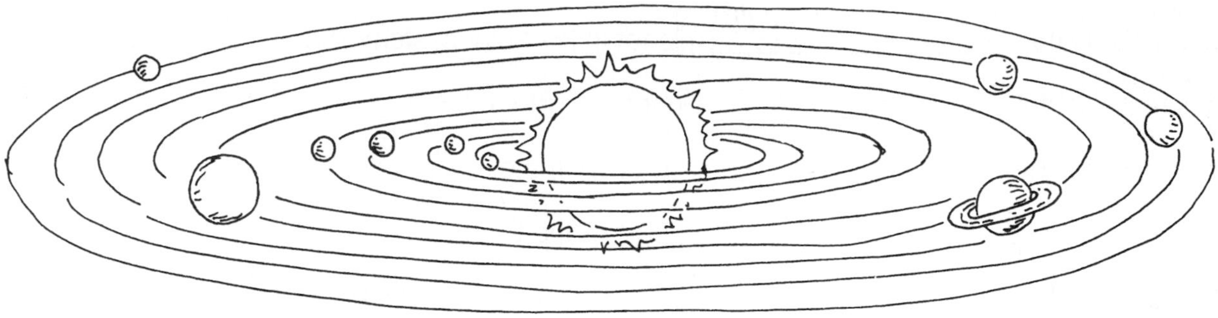

The Solar System

The Sun ______________________________

Mercury ______________________________

Venus ______________________________

Earth ______________________________

The Moon ______________________________

Jupiter ______________________________

Uranus ______________________________

Neptune ______________________________

Name ____

Superlatives

Fill in the sentences with the superlative form of each word given. The superlative form ends in *-est.*

1. Mercury is the ____closest____ planet to the Sun. (close)
2. Jupiter is the ________________ planet in the solar system. (big)
3. Venus is the ________________ planet to Earth. (close)
4. Venus has the ________________ rotation in the solar system. (slow)
5. The core is the ________________ part of the Sun. (hot)
6. Pluto is the ________________ planet in the solar system. (small)
7. Pluto is also the ________________ planet in the solar system. (cold)
8. Jupiter's moon Europa is the ________________ object in the solar system. (smooth)
9. Neptune's moon Triton is the ________________ place in the solar system. (cold)
10. Venus is the ________________ planet in the solar system. (hot)
11. Jupiter has the ________________ rotation of the planets. (fast)
12. Pluto has the ________________ year in the solar system. (long)

Name ____

Space Idioms

Complete the sentences with the idioms in the Word Bank.
These idioms are on page 152 of the Student Book.

Word Bank
spaced out
sunny-side up
out of this world
sitting on top of the world

1. Angela's new hat is ______________________________!
2. Margie didn't hear what I said because she was ______________________________.
3. I've been ______________________________ since I won the swimming trophy.
4. Why did you scramble my eggs? I like them ______________________________.

Here are four new idioms with space words. Can you guess what they mean by studying the words around them? Draw a line from each idiom to its meaning.

1. Lobster is expensive. So I only eat it *once in a blue moon.*

2. Juan is *starry eyed* over his new girlfriend.

3. That is the best chocolate *under the sun!*

4. Vanessa hates to lose. She will *move heaven and earth* to win first prize in the spelling contest.

very much in love with

rarely, not very often

do anything; work very hard

on Earth; anywhere

Name ______________________________

Science Objective: Demonstrate the ability to relate or apply scientific and technological information to daily life.

Clues

1. When you take tests, some questions will ask you to relate scientific principles to daily life.
2. Many questions will ask you to apply scientific and technological information to explain natural processes or phenomena. Some will ask you to solve problems or make predictions based on information given.

Sample

This chart shows phases of the moon.

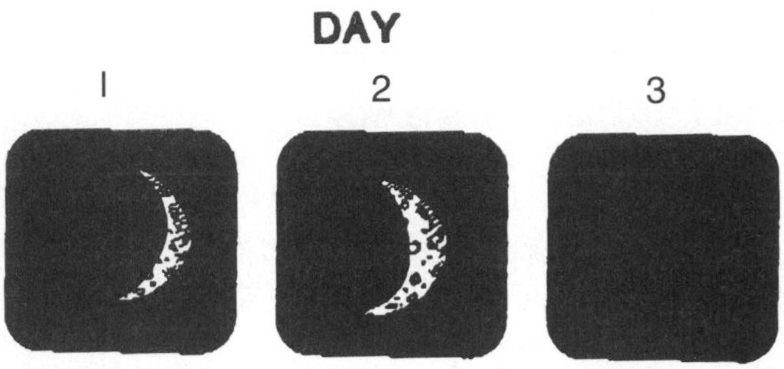

Which shows the phase for the third day?

A. 

C. 

B. 

D. 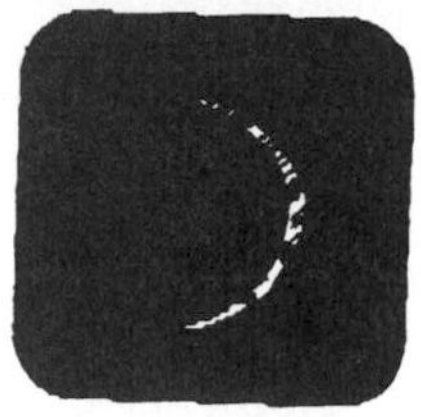

If you chose answer C, you are right!

Name ____

Try It

Read each question carefully. Mark the circle next to the correct answer.

1. If a telescope is focused on the moon and the moon slowly disappears, what is the reasonable explanation?
   - ○ The moon moved away.
   - ○ The earth rotated on its axis.
   - ○ The moon was overpowered by a star.
   - ○ The moon was orbiting the Sun.

2. According to the chart below, which candy bar would you choose if you wanted the lowest fat content?
   - ○ Bar 1
   - ○ Bar 2
   - ○ Bar 3
   - ○ Bar 4

Candy Bar	Calories	Carbohydrates	Fat	Cholesterol	Potassium
Bar 1	150	18 g	26 g	14 mg	60 mg
Bar 2	165	14 g	18 g	11 mg	90 mg
Bar 3	190	17 g	22 g	12 mg	0 mg
Bar 4	240	15 g	14 g	9 mg	8 mg

For questions 3 and 4, look at the chart on pages 134 and 135 of the Student Book.

3. According to the chart, which planet takes the longest to make one orbit of the Sun?
   - ○ Pluto
   - ○ Earth
   - ○ Mars
   - ○ Neptune

4. Which planet takes the most time to make one rotation?
   - ○ Venus
   - ○ Mars
   - ○ Earth
   - ○ Mercury

Name ______________________________

Proofread and Correct

These sentences contain place names that should be capitalized. Proofread the sentences. Rewrite them to show the correct capital letters.

1. The united states changed greatly during the 1800s and early 1900s.

   ____

2. Before 1800, most people lived between the atlantic ocean and the appalachian mountains.

   ____

   ____

3. Eventually, settlers moved across the mississippi river and went as far as the pacific ocean.

   ____

   ____

4. Many of the settlers had been born in europe.

   ____

5. They settled in areas that later became states, such as minnesota, nebraska, and iowa.

   ____

   ____

Complete the sentences.

1. I live in the city of ______________________________.
2. I live in the state of ______________________________.
3. The nearest river is the ______________________________.
4. The name of the country I came from is ______________________________.

Name ______________________________

Map Reading

The map below shows the years when the states west of the Mississippi River became part of the United States.

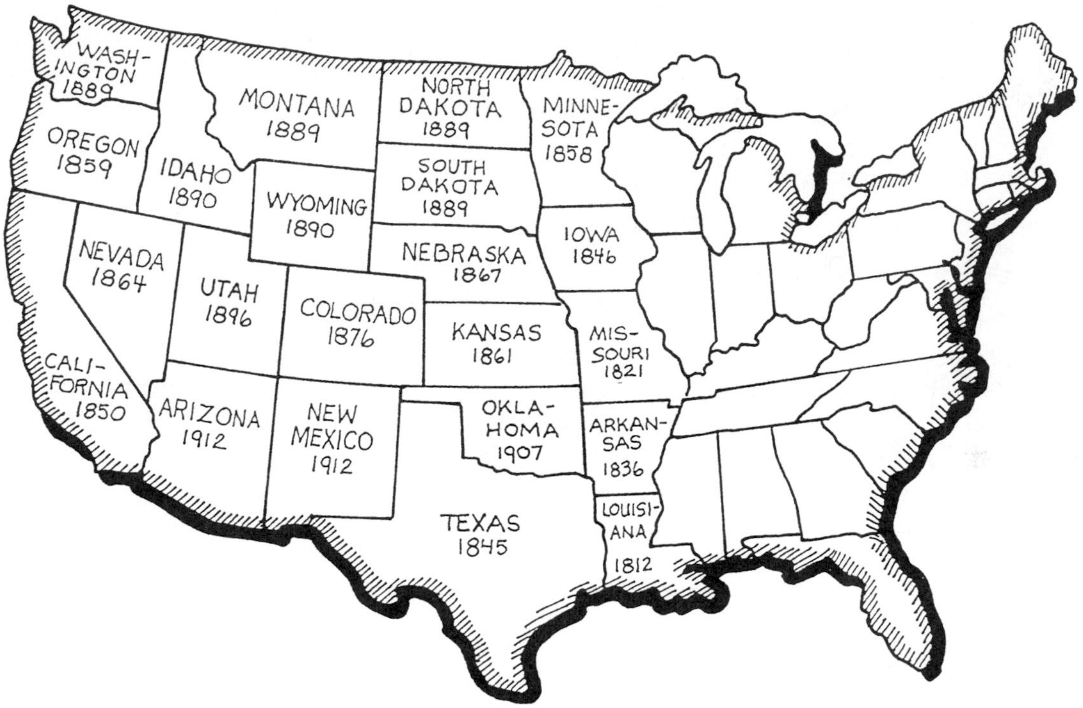

Use the map to answer the questions.

1. How many states were added to the United States in the following decades?

1840s ______ 1850s ______ 1860s ______

1870s ______ 1880s ______ 1890s ______

1900s ______ 1910s ______

2. In which year were the most states added to the United States? How many states were added?

____

3. What states were added in that year?

____

4. Which were the last states on the map to be added to the United States? When were they added?

____

Name ______________________________

United States: Past and Present

Complete the sentences with words that end in *-less*. Use the underlined words as clues.

1. People thought that they could not put the land in the West to use. They thought the land was ______________.

2. Some places in the West had no trees. These places were ______________.

3. People wanted to own land. They moved from the East because they were ______________.

4. Settlers needed to be without fear to face the dangers of the long trip west. They needed to be ______________.

5. Before the 1900s, carriages with horses were used to carry people. The first cars were called ______________ carriages because they did not use horses.

6. One problem in the United States today is people who have no homes. These people are ______________.

7. People now know that the environment must be kept clean. They treat the environment with care. They are not ______________.

8. Computers have become very important to business. People can no longer imagine a society that is ______________.

Name ______________________________

Settling the West

Complete the sentences by writing the passive voice of the verbs in parentheses.

During the 1800s, the West ___was settled___ (settle) by Europeans and others looking for a better life. The settlers traveled in large wagons. The wagons ______________ (pull) by horses or oxen. The wagon tops ______________ (cover) with cloth to keep out the sun. When a large group of families and their wagons traveled together, the group ______________ (call) a wagon train.

American Indians had already lived in the West for thousands of years. As the settlers moved west, they fought with the Indians. After many years, the Indians ______________ (defeat). Then they ______________ (force) to live in areas the settlers did not want.

Wherever the settlers went, towns ______________ (create). The grasslands ______________ (turn) into ranches. Fields ______________ (plant). In 1869, a transcontinental railroad ______________ (complete). More cities and farms ______________ (start) along the railway. Soon the West ______________ (fill) with settlers.

Name ______________________________

Prairie or Forest?

Put each item in the correct category, prairie or forest.

beaver	many kinds of grass
buffalo	many kinds of trees
corn	maples
deer	much precipitation
farmers	oats
few trees	owls
little precipitation	wheat

Prairie	Forest

Name ______________________________

Word Search

Find the words in the puzzle and circle them.

Word Bank

BUFFALO	GRASSLAND	OWL	SETTLER
DEER	MAPLE TREE	PRAIRIE	WAGON
FOREST	OAK TREE	PRECIPITATION	WHEAT

G	P	K	W	L	V	N	U	J	D	E	E	R	A	T
B	H	R	I	F	U	S	F	D	U	O	S	I	E	U
M	U	G	E	E	D	A	T	F	H	A	R	K	S	H
A	T	R	O	C	M	G	J	O	A	K	T	R	E	E
P	H	I	F	L	I	S	O	R	K	Q	C	G	T	E
L	M	G	D	C	N	P	K	E	O	D	O	A	T	O
E	I	L	G	K	L	B	I	S	J	S	F	R	L	M
T	T	W	H	E	A	T	P	T	M	I	Q	O	E	Z
R	J	E	A	I	N	A	B	Q	A	N	U	P	R	N
E	U	F	R	D	P	C	C	V	L	T	R	E	U	Y
E	I	F	R	O	I	P	I	K	O	I	I	X	A	B
W	D	D	E	W	C	L	R	E	Y	U	V	O	B	L
V	G	C	P	L	F	G	R	A	S	S	L	A	N	D
B	H	N	A	B	A	O	W	V	I	T	P	K	T	I
T	W	A	G	O	N	H	E	A	M	R	E	R	W	O
Y	A	O	B	A	C	E	Z	A	C	S	I	E	I	X
X	I	T	B	U	F	F	A	L	O	Z	L	E	R	T

Name ______________________________

Who am I?

Read the descriptions of the characters in the story *Sarah, Plain and Tall*. Then write the name of each character by his or her description.

Characters
Anna
Caleb
Papa
Sarah

Descriptions

1. I drove the wagon to get Sarah. ____________
2. I rocked on the porch as I waited. ____________
3. I liked my new shell. ____________
4. I climbed up on the porch roof and tried to see the wagon better. ____________
5. I had a pet cat named Seal. ____________
6. I watched the sheep and the cows and the hawk as I waited. ____________
7. I thought the prairie land rolled a little like the sea. ____________
8. I washed my face clean but not too clean. ____________
9. I fed and watered the horses and hitched them to the wagon. ____________
10. I thought the sea stone was the smoothest and whitest stone I had ever seen.

____

Name ______________________________

Sound Search

Circle each word that contains the sound of long *o.* Remember, this sound may be spelled *o, oa,* or *ow.*

1. Old Bess was calm and kind. “Clear day, Bess,” said Papa, rubbing her nose. And then Papa drove off down the road.

2. “I know she will be nice,” I told Caleb as we waited for Papa to bring Sarah home.

3. Sarah gave Caleb a shell. She said the gulls fly high and drop the shells on the rocks below. Then she gave me the smoothest and whitest stone I had ever seen. I showed it to Caleb.

4. The settlers hoped for a better life. They wanted to have land and grow wheat and oats.

5. In the West, the settlers found several biomes. Huge herds of buffalo roamed the grassy prairie. In the forest were many kinds of trees, such as oaks and maples. Cold streams flowed in the shade.

Name ____

Social Studies Objective: Demonstrate an understanding of geographical concepts and information.

Clues

1. When you take tests, questions for this objective will ask you to describe the geographic regions of your state, the United States, and the world in terms of physical, cultural, and economic features.
2. Some questions will ask you to analyze the influence of natural resources on the development of the United States.

Samples

1. Which of these was a physical barrier to settlers moving west?

   A. the Great Lakes

   B. the Mississippi River

   C. the Atlantic Ocean

   D. the Rio Grande

B is correct! The Mississippi River later became a great water route for people who wanted to travel north and south, but it was a barrier that had to be crossed for settlers who wanted to go west.

2. During their journeys west, settlers often encountered

   A. leopards

   B. camels

   C. buffalo

   D. llamas

Did you choose C? Of the four animals listed, only buffalo are native to North America.

Name ______________________________

Try It

Read each question carefully. Mark the circle next to the answer.

1. Which of the following mountains did settlers going from the eastern U.S. to the West encounter?
   - ○ The Rocky Mountains
   - ○ The Andes Mountains
   - ○ The Pyrenees Mountains
   - ○ The Himalayas

2. The desert was an obstacle when going from Texas to California because
   - ○ it had cactus
   - ○ many dangerous wild animals lived there
   - ○ it offered very few sources of food and fresh water
   - ○ it had many earthquakes

3. Texas is a leading oil-producing state. Oil is a nonrenewable resource. Which of the following is also a nonrenewable resource?
   - ○ Timber
   - ○ Gold
   - ○ Wheat
   - ○ Dairy products

4. Which geographical feature could be described as a "sea of grass"?
   - ○ A mountain range
   - ○ A prairie
   - ○ A river delta
   - ○ A desert

Name ______________________________

Inventions

Write the name of each invention under its picture. Use the words in the box.

Word Bank		
camera	light bulb	steam engine
car	telephone	typewriter

1. 1876

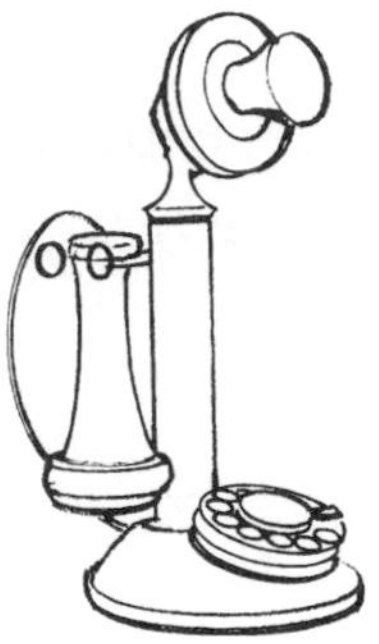

____

2. 1867

____

3. 1879

____

4. 1839

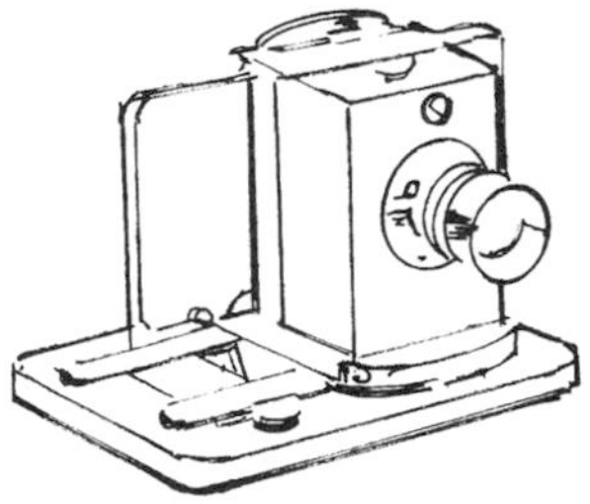

____

5. 1885

____

6. 1804

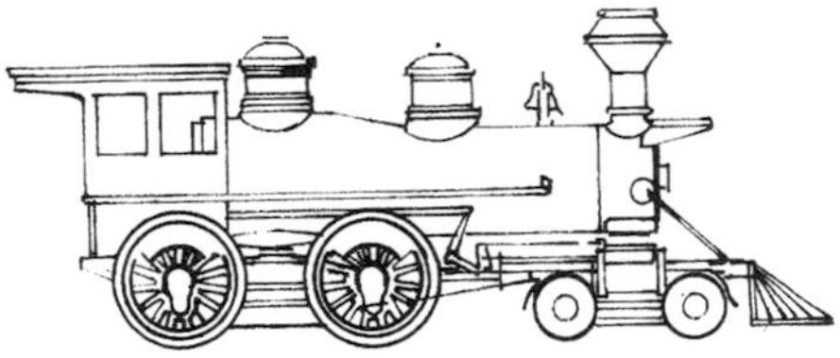

____

Complete the following sentences. Use *before, after,* or *during.*

1. ______________ the 1800s, the car and the steam engine were invented.
2. The steam engine was invented ______________ the car.
3. The car was invented ______________ the camera.
4. The car was invented ______________ the telephone.

Name ______________________________

Inventors and Reformers

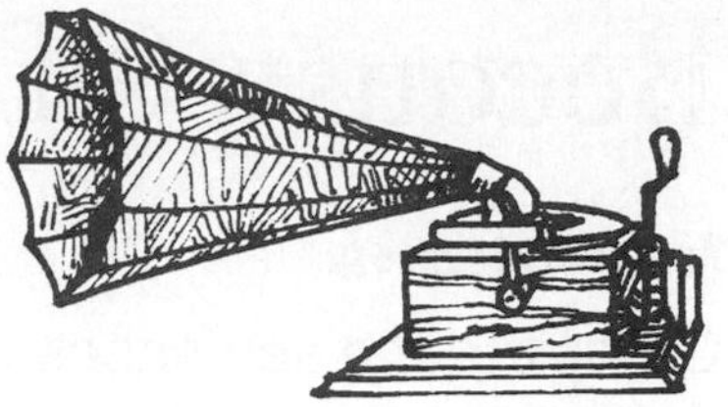

Add the phrase in parentheses to the sentence. Write the new sentence on the line.

1. Alexander Graham Bell invented the telephone. (an immigrant from Scotland)

   Alexander Graham Bell, an immigrant from Scotland, invented the telephone.

2. Henry Ford invented the assembly line. (a way to build cars quickly and cheaply)

   ____

   ____

3. Thomas Edison invented the light bulb. (one of the world's most famous inventors)

   ____

   ____

4. The Standard Oil Company was headed by John D. Rockefeller. (a large and powerful company)

   ____

   ____

5. Ida Tarbell thought that John D. Rockefeller got unfair deals from others. (a writer)

   ____

   ____

6. Upton Sinclair helped to change the meat packing business. (a novelist)

   ____

   ____

Name ________________________________

Because Of

Inventions

Complete the sentences with phrases that begin with *because of.* Use the information you learned in this unit.

1. Because of the phonograph ______________________,
   people could listen to music in their homes.
2. ______________________,
   people could write letters more quickly and easily.
3. ______________________,
   people could have light at all times of day cheaply and easily.
4. ______________________,
   people could get pictures of themselves and important events in their lives.
5. ______________________,
   people could travel from one place to another more easily.
6. ______________________,
   people could talk to other people in different parts of the city or country.
7. ______________________,
   cars could be made more quickly.

People

Complete the sentences. Use *because of* and the phrases in the box.

Info Box
Sinclair's writing
Ford's assembly line

1. ______________________, meat was packed more safely.
2. ______________________, cars were made more cheaply.

Name ________________________________

Reading Graphs

The graph shows how many Americans were living in urban and rural areas between 1870 and 1920. Use information from the graph to answer the questions.

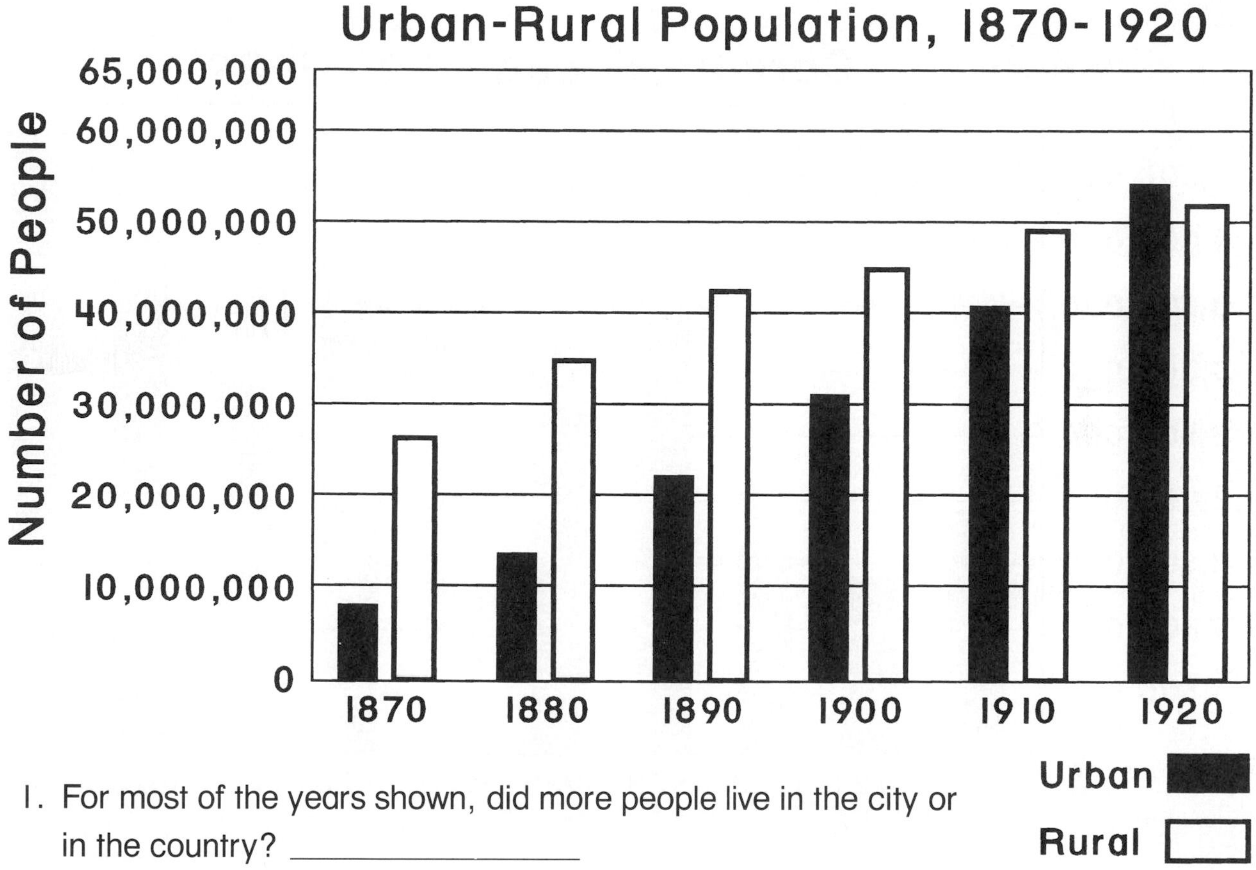

1. For most of the years shown, did more people live in the city or in the country? ______________
2. As you follow the graph from left to right, which group seems to be growing faster? ______________
3. By which year did the urban population become greater than the rural population? ______________
4. Did either group, rural or urban, lose population between 1870 and 1920? ______________
5. From 1870 to 1900, did the urban population grow more or less than the rural population? Give approximate numbers.

____

____

Name ______________________________

Ask the questions.

The United States grew rapidly as an industrial nation. Look at the following graph. It shows the number of cars that factories in the United States made during the 1920s. Write questions that go with the answers.

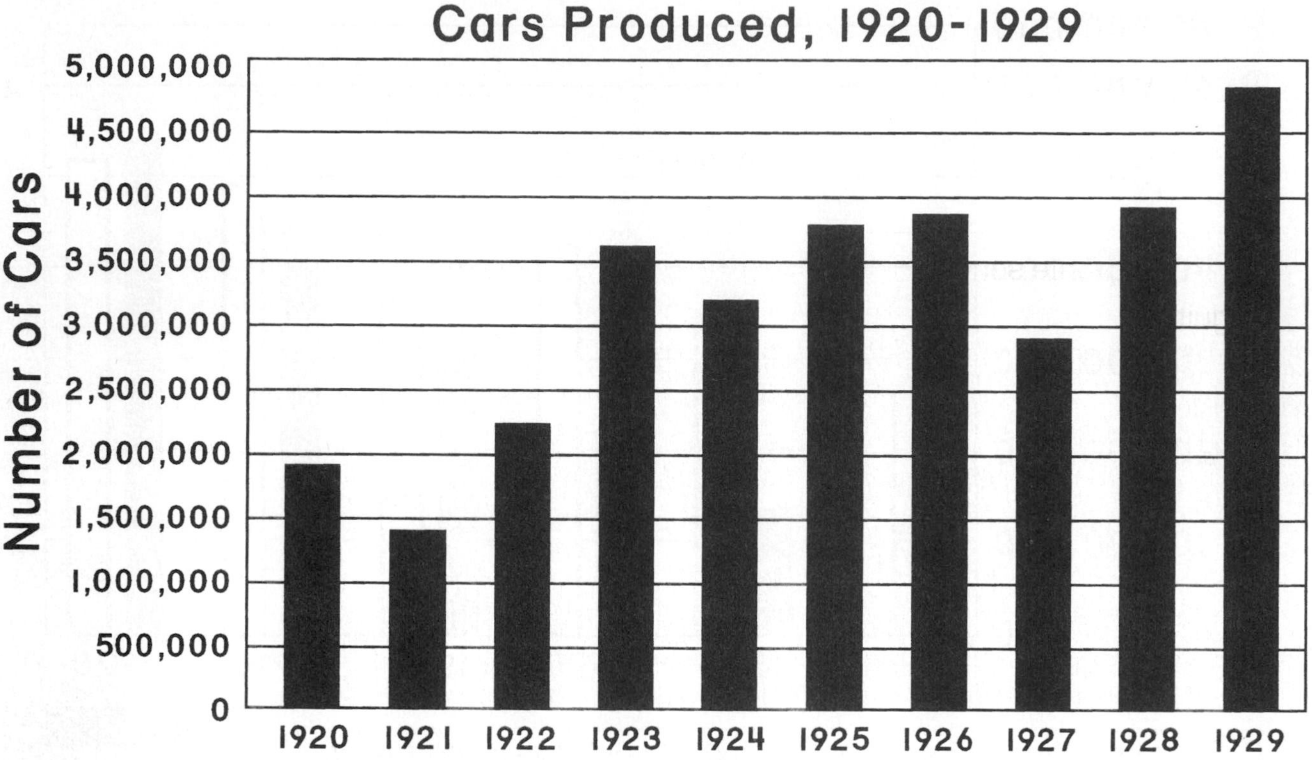

1. How many cars did factories produce in 1921?
   Factories produced almost 1,500,000 cars.

2. ______________________________
   Factories produced almost 5,000,000 cars.

3. ______________________________
   Car production decreased in 1921, 1924, and 1927.

4. ______________________________
   Factories first produced over 3,000,000 cars in 1923.

5. ______________________________
   Your own answer:
   ____

Name ______________________

If . . .

Unscramble the words to form sentences with if.

1. a jet plane \ if I had \ I would buy \ a million dollars

   If I had a million dollars, I would buy a jet plane.

2. a lot of money \ if I were rich \ I would give away

   ____

3. all my favorite songs \ if I knew \ I would play \ how to play the guitar

   ____

Complete the sentences to tell what you would do in each situation.

1. If I were twenty-one years old, ______________________
2. If I were in high school, ______________________
3. If I could go anywhere in the world, ______________________
4. If I had 10 million dollars, ______________________
5. If I were President of the United States, ______________________
6. If I could change two things, ______________________

Name ______________________________

Crossword Puzzle

Use the words in the box to complete the puzzle.

Across

1. After he wrote about the meat packing industry, the government passed new laws to make food safer.
4. She was a reformer who criticized the way Rockefeller did business.
6. He was the head of a giant oil company.
7. He gave away almost $350 million during the last 18 years of his life.
8. He bought Carnegie's steel properties for half a billion dollars.

Bell	Industrial	Morgan	Rockefeller	steel
Carnegie	inventors	reform	Sinclair	Tarbell

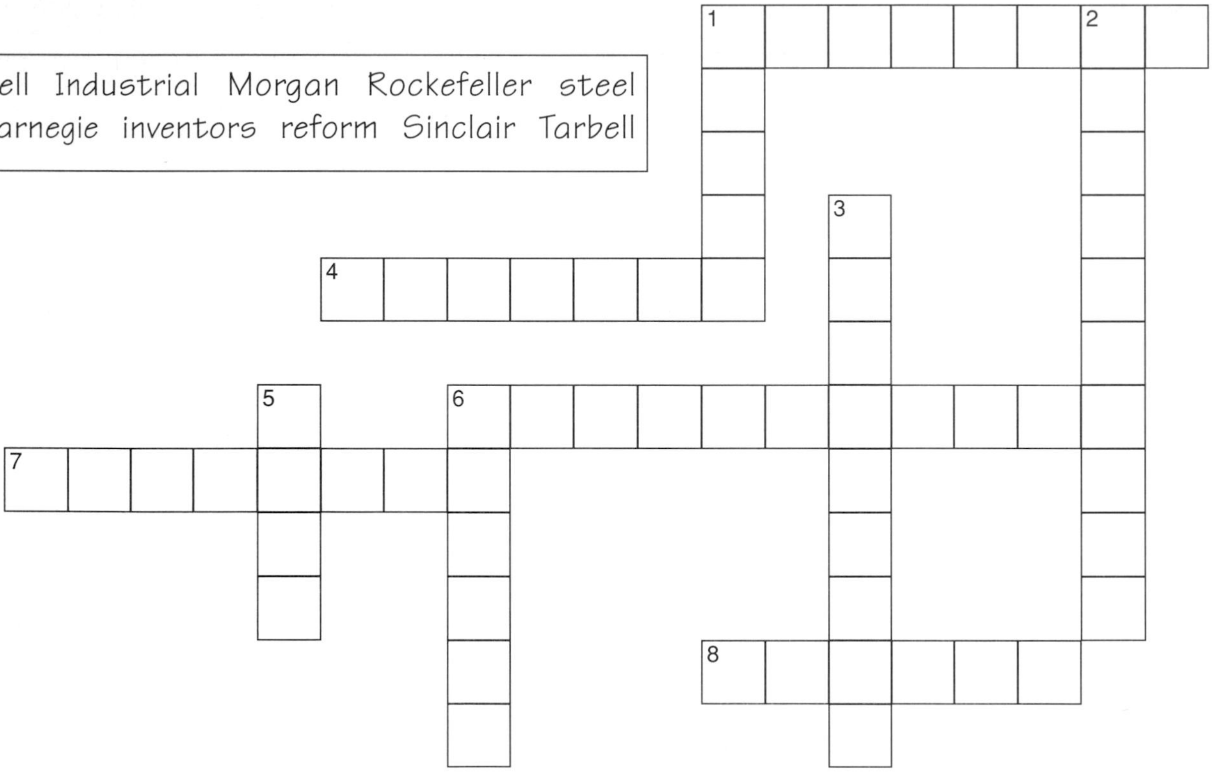

Down

1. Carnegie made much of his money in the ______ industry.
2. The ______ Revolution caused many changes in the United States.
3. Thomas Edison, Alexander Graham Bell, and Henry Ford were famous ______.
5. He was the Scottish immigrant who invented the telephone.
6. The ______ movement helped change the way big companies did business.

Name ____________________

Can you help?

Look at the pictures. What is the person saying? Complete the requests. Begin with either *Can you?* or *Could you?*

Info Box	
give me change for a dollar	show me a book about settlers in the West
tell me the time	give me directions
carry this for me	give me a piece of paper

1.

2.

3.

4.

5.

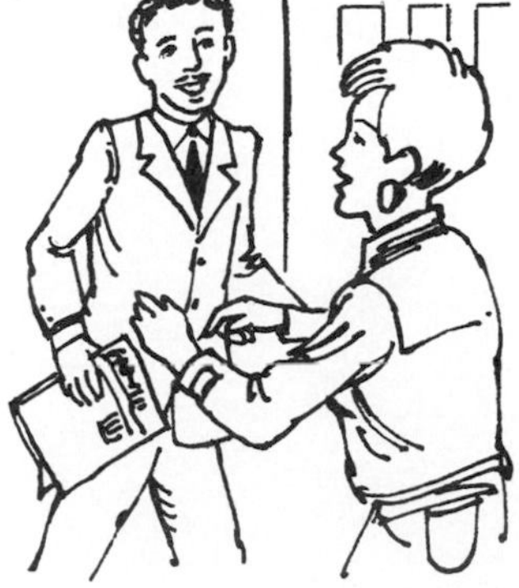

6.

Name ____

Writing Objectives: Recognize appropriate sentence construction within the context of a written message.

Recognize appropriate English usage within the context of a written passage.

Recognize appropriate spelling, capitalization, and punctuation within the context of a written passage.

Clues

1. When you take tests, read carefully to determine the best choice to replace incomplete sentences, run-on sentences, or errors in subject-verb agreement.
2. Identify spelling, capitalization, or punctuation errors. You will not have to correct them.

Samples

People need <u>jobs for many reasons.</u> People <u>liked working sew they could</u> buy more things.

1. Identify the mistake in phrase 1 in the box above.

   A. Spelling

   B. Capitalization

   C. Punctuation

   D. No mistake

If you chose "D, No mistake," for number 1, you are correct. There are no errors in spelling, capitalization, or punctuation.

2. Identify the mistake in phrase 2 in the box above.

   A. Spelling

   B. Capitalization

   C. Punctuation

   D. No mistake

Number 2 has a spelling error: *sew* should be *so*. The correct answer is A.

Name ______________________________

Try It

Read each question carefully. Mark the circle next to the correct answer.

> During the 1800, thousands of people left their farms, they came to the city. (1) Most people begin to work (2) in the factories. Before, this time, (3) people made things by hand. The United States changed greatly during the Industrial Revolution. (4)

1. In the box above, how should phrase 1 read?
   - ○ During the 1800s, thousands of people left their farms. They came to the city.
   - ○ During the 1800, thousands of people left their farms. They came to the city.
   - ○ During the 1800s, thousands of people left their farms, they came to the city.
   - ○ No mistake

2. How should phrase 2 read?
   - ○ begin working
   - ○ nonworking
   - ○ began to work
   - ○ No mistake

3. Identify the mistake in phrase 3.
   - ○ Spelling
   - ○ Capitalization
   - ○ Punctuation
   - ○ No mistake

4. Identify the mistake in phrase 4.
   - ○ Spelling
   - ○ Capitalization
   - ○ Punctuation
   - ○ No mistake

Name ______________________________

Facts About Population ★★★★

Every ten years the government of the United States counts the number of people who live in the country. Study the list. Answer the questions.

Population of the United States, 1790-1990

Year	People
1790	3,929,000
1800	5,308,000
1810	7,240,000
1820	9,638,000
1830	12,861,000
1840	17,063,000
1850	23,192,000
1860	31,443,000
1870	38,558,000
1880	50,189,000
1890	62,980,000
1900	76,212,000
1910	92,228,000
1920	106,022,000
1930	123,203,000
1940	132,165,000
1950	151,326,000
1960	179,323,000
1970	203,302,000
1980	226,542,000
1990	248,710,000

1. In what year did the United States have the largest population?

   ____

2. In what year did the United States have the smallest population?

   ____

3. By what year had the U.S. population passed 100,000,000?

   ____

4. In what year was the U.S. population about 76,000,000?

   ____

5. By what year had the U.S. population passed 200,000,000?

   ____

6. Abraham Lincoln was elected President of the United States in 1860. About how many people lived here then?

   ____

7. Ronald Reagan was elected President of the United States in 1980. About how many people lived here then?

   ____

Name ____

The Pledge of Allegiance

Read the Pledge of Allegiance. This is a basic statement of a person's loyalty to the United States.

> I pledge Allegiance to the flag of the United States of America, and to the Republic for which it stands, one nation, under God, indivisible, with liberty and justice for all.

Find the words below from the pledge in the puzzle. Circle them.

ALLEGIANCE	JUSTICE
AMERICA	LIBERTY
FLAG	NATION
GOD	REPUBLIC

M	F	N	R	O	E	S	Q	X	I
A	L	L	E	G	I	A	N	C	E
M	A	E	P	F	D	V	H	R	N
E	G	J	U	S	T	I	C	E	A
R	C	X	B	T	G	O	D	Q	T
I	P	K	L	X	L	K	D	F	I
C	T	L	I	B	E	R	T	Y	O
A	S	V	C	H	S	O	F	P	N

Name ____

Becoming a Citizen

Study the list. Use the facts to write complete sentences about becoming a citizen. Use *have to* or *must* in each sentence.

Naturalized Citizens

- speak English
- live here for 5 years
- be at least 18 years old
- support the United States above all others
- know about U.S. history and government

____

____

____

____

____

In school, you must follow certain rules. List three of them here. Use complete sentences.

____

____

____

____

____

____

____

____

____

____

Name ______________________________

Duties of a Citizen

Classify the duties and rights of a citizen. Put each item in the box in the correct column. Some may go into both columns.

equality before the law	freedom of speech
obeying the laws of the nation	being on a jury
paying taxes	respecting the rights of others
voting	ability to own property

Duties of a Citizen	**Rights of a Citizen**
______________________	______________________
______________________	______________________
______________________	______________________
______________________	______________________
______________________	______________________

Find the words in the box in the puzzle. Circle them.

CITIZENS	FAIRNESS	RESPONSIBILITIES	RIGHTS
TAXES	TRUTH	VOTING	

F	J	C	I	T	I	Z	E	N	S	X	B	P	X	P	M
A	K	P	L	M	I	E	T	S	K	V	O	T	I	N	G
I	E	J	V	H	B	O	R	S	I	L	J	M	B	T	V
R	E	S	P	O	N	S	I	B	I	L	I	T	I	E	S
N	V	T	O	J	K	T	G	E	B	O	E	A	T	K	L
E	T	R	M	X	D	C	H	F	G	D	N	X	Q	C	H
S	L	K	Q	T	R	U	T	H	T	H	A	E	Q	R	S
S	M	V	E	H	O	V	S	F	K	F	J	S	T	O	B

Name ____

Being a Good Citizen

Read the sentences. Write in the correct word forms. Use words ending in *-ing.* Be sure to spell them correctly.

(Be) ______________ a good citizen is important. It means (respect) ______________ the rights of others. It means (pay) ______________ taxes on time. It means (vote) ______________ in all elections. It means (tell) ______________ the truth in court, and (help) ______________ others when they need it. (Be) ______________ a good citizen means (care) ______________ about the future of the United States and (do) ______________ what you can for the good of all.

Write what being a good citizen means to you.

____

____

____

____

____

____

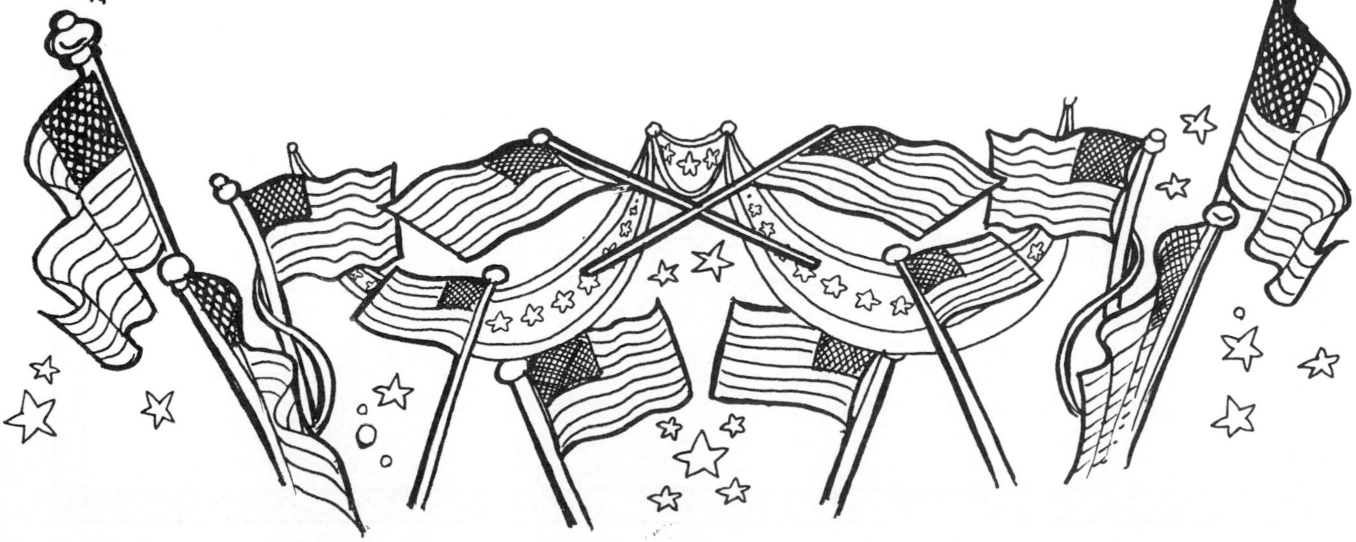

Name ____________________

Immigrants and Naturalized Citizens

Study the table. Fill in the blanks.

Immigrants and Naturalized Citizens, 1930 to 1980

Years	Immigrants	Naturalized Citizens
1930s	528,431	1,518,464
1940s	1,035,039	1,987,028
1950s	2,515,479	1,189,946
1960s	3,321,677	1,120,263
1970s	4,493,314	1,464,772

This table shows how many immigrants entered the United States between ____________ and ____________. The fewest immigrants came to the United States during the decade of the ____________. This small number was because of the hard economic times in the United States and other places in the world during those years. Many of the 1,518,464 people who became naturalized citizens during the ____________ arrived before that time. The greatest number of immigrants came to the United States in the ____________. But the greatest number of people became naturalized citizens during the ____________. The fewest people became naturalized citizens during the ____________.

Name ____

Words to Know

Use the clues to fill in the crossword puzzle.

Across

3. woman who wrote a poem that says, "Give me your tired, your poor"
4. place where the Statue of Liberty and Ellis Island are located
5. people of this nation sent a gift to the people of the United States
6. size of the island on which the Statue of Liberty is located
8. place where poor immigrants were admitted to the United States

Down

1. name of a famous U.S. symbol
2. people who were admitted to the U.S. through Ellis Island
7. what Ellis Island is today
9. what the Statue of Liberty holds in her outstretched hand

Name ______________________________

Letters from Rifka

These sentences are based on the story "Letters from Rifka." Some sentences are incorrect. Rewrite the incorrect sentences to make them correct.

1. Rifka was immigrating to the United States from Poland.

   Rifka was immigrating to the United States from Russia.

2. Rifka was crossing the Pacific Ocean.

   ____

3. Rifka had never seen some of her brothers.

   ____

4. Rifka was writing the letter on Ellis Island.

   ____

5. Rifka was afraid about answering the questions at Ellis Island.

   ____

6. The trip across the ocean seemed fast to Rifka.

   ____

7. To Rifka, the United States was a place to begin a new life.

   ____

8. Rifka saw the Statue of Liberty from the ship.

   ____

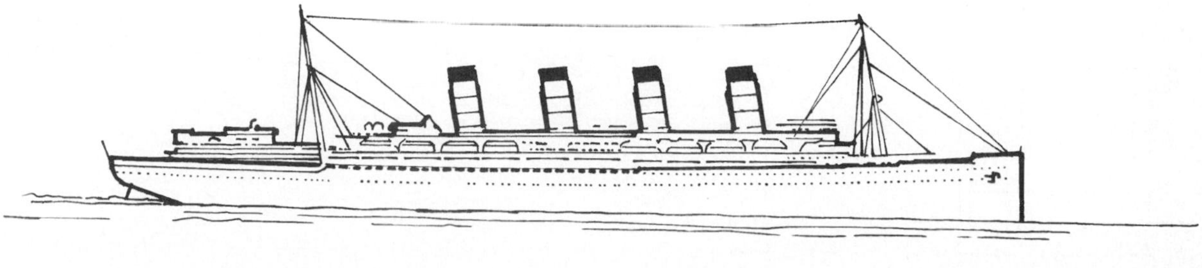

Name ____

Reading Objectives: Analyze information in a variety of written texts in order to make inferences and generalizations.

Recognize points of view, propaganda, and/or statements of fact and nonfact in a variety of written texts.

Clues

1. When you take tests, information may be in a graph, chart, or directly in the passage. Make sure you know what the question is asking you to find.
2. Some of the questions will ask you to decide between fact or nonfact. A fact is something that can be proven. You can look back in the passage to review the facts the author gives.

Sample

A citizen is a person who is a member of a nation. There are two ways to become a citizen. One is to be born in a country, and the other is to choose to live there. Many United States citizens have chosen the United States as their home. They came from many other countries. When people move to a new country, they are called immigrants.

Which of these is NOT a fact in the passage?

A. You can be a citizen by being born in a country.

B. You have to be 21 years old to become a citizen.

C. People who move from one country to another are immigrants.

D. A citizen is a member of a nation.

Did you choose B? That's right. This statement was not a fact given in the passage.

Name ____________________

Try It

Read the passage. Mark the circle next to the correct answer for each question.

"Give Me Your Tired . . ."

The Statue of Liberty is a symbol of what people hope to find in the United States: fairness, equality, opportunity, and freedom. Its right hand and torch were given to the United States in 1876 by the people of France as a 100-year birthday present. The giant statue was completed in 1884. Then it was placed on a tiny island in New York Harbor to welcome immigrants. It was the best gift the United States could have received from any country.

1. Which statement is an opinion stated in the passage?
   - ○ The statue was placed in New York Harbor.
   - ○ The Statue of Liberty was a birthday present.
   - ○ France gave part of the statue to the U. S. in 1876.
   - ○ It was the best gift the U. S. could have received.

2. The author probably wrote this passage in order to
   - ○ inform people about immigration
   - ○ tell how many people have come through Ellis Island
   - ○ tell about the meaning of the Statue of Liberty
   - ○ explain about citizens

Use the immigration chart on page 200 of the Student Book to answer questions 3 and 4.

3. According to the chart, which decade welcomed the most immigrants?
   - ○ 1980s
   - ○ 1900s
   - ○ 1940s
   - ○ 1910s

4. The lowest number of immigrants in any decade shown on the chart is
   - ○ 1,035,039
   - ○ 5,735,811
   - ○ 528, 431
   - ○ 2,515,479

Name ______________________________

The First Amendment

Read about the First Amendment.

Amendment 1

The government cannot pass laws that make any religion the official religion of the country. The government cannot make laws that stop people from speaking and writing what they wish. It cannot make laws that stop people from holding peaceful meetings or from asking the government to correct a wrong.

Write *Yes* for the examples that would involve the First Amendment. Write *No* for the examples that would not involve the First Amendment.

___Yes___ 1. The government passes a law that says only certain people can make speeches about health care issues.

__________ 2. The government passes a law that says all people must pay more taxes.

__________ 3. The government passes a law that changes where the border is between the states of Texas and Louisiana.

__________ 4. Some neighbors get together to talk about the amount of crime in their neighborhood.

__________ 5. People decide themselves which church they want to go to.

__________ 6. A young person decides to join the U.S. Army after graduating from high school.

__________ 7. A company decides to sell its products for less money.

__________ 8. A parent writes a letter to the editor of the newspaper in support of plans to build a new high school in town.

Name ______________________________

Which Branch of Government?

Read the list. Then match the items with the three branches of government.

makes the laws
approves the laws
hears court cases
has 100 senators
is headed by the President
has 9 members
meets with leaders of other countries
decides if laws are constitutional
has 435 representatives

Legislative

____

____

____

____

____

Executive

____

____

____

____

____

Judicial

____

____

____

____

____

Name ______________________________

The Branches of Government

Use the clues to complete the crossword puzzle.

Across

2. where the President lives
3. name for the part of Congress with 100 members
6. how many Presidents there can be
7. name for the part of Congress with 435 members

Down

1. name for the highest court in the country
2. name of the first U.S. President
4. the number of branches of government
5. what Congress makes

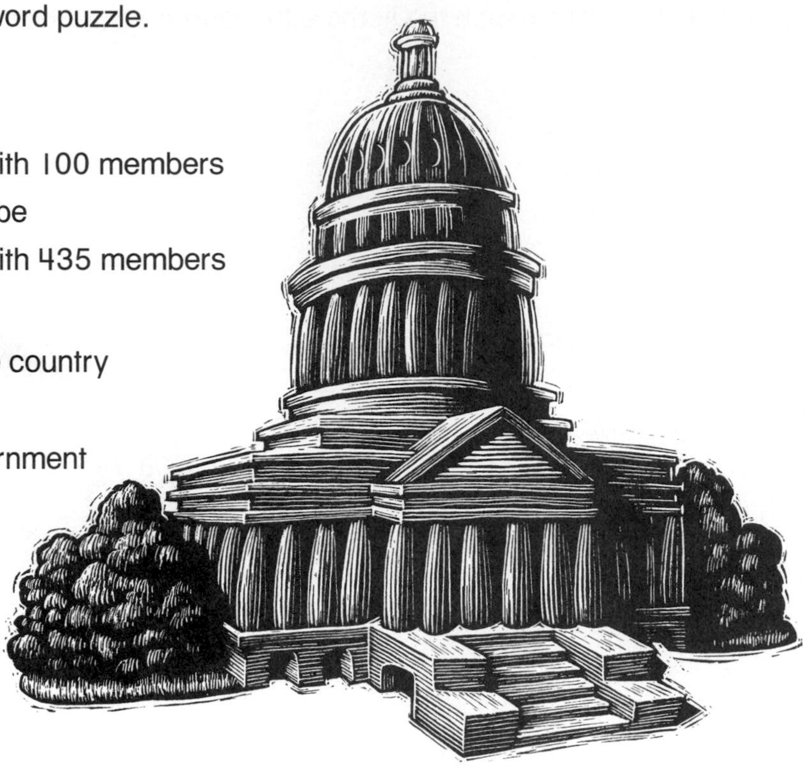

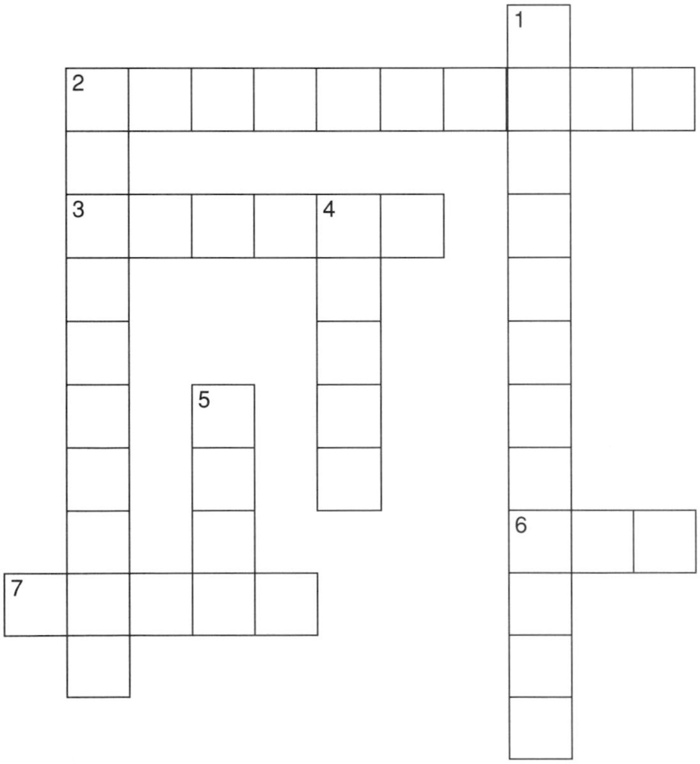

Name ______________________________

The President

Read the list. Then write each item in the correct category.

must be 35 years old
heads the executive branch
meets with leaders of other countries
must have been born in the United States
can be either a man or woman
lives in the White House
can come from any political party
is commander in chief of the military

Requirements for Being President

____

____

____

____

The Role of President

____

____

____

____

Use the lines below to tell what kind of person you think would make a good President.

____

____

____

____

____

____

____

____

____

____

Name ____________________

Since When?

Study the time line about the history of the United States. Write sentences that follow the example. Use *since* in your answers.

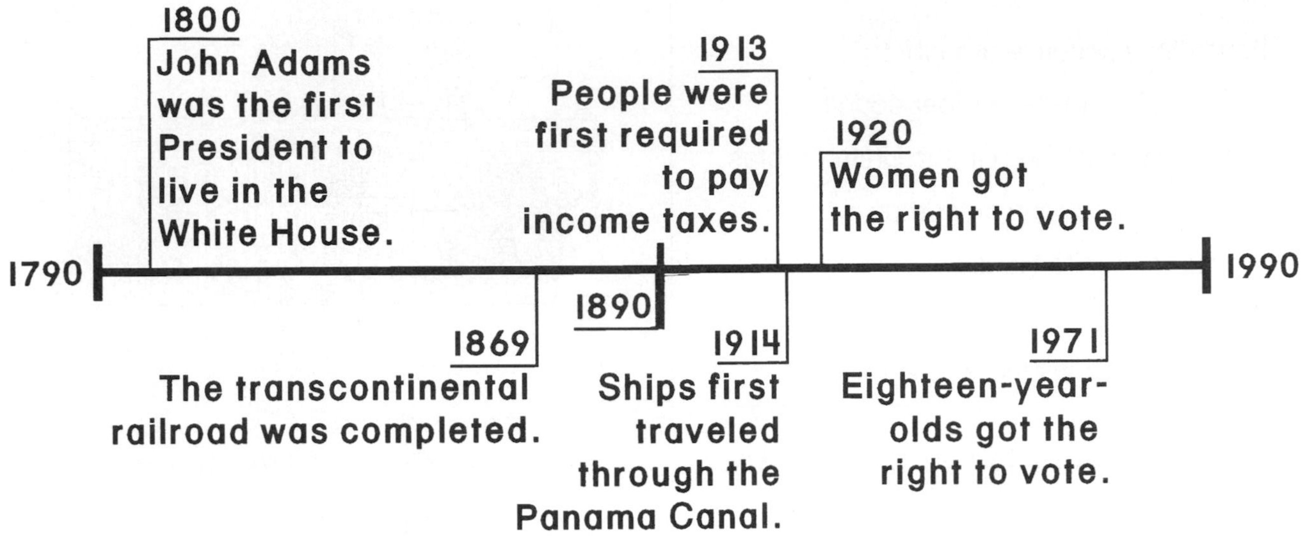
1790
1800 John Adams was the first President to live in the White House.
1869 The transcontinental railroad was completed.
1890
1913 People were first required to pay income taxes.
1914 Ships first traveled through the Panama Canal.
1920 Women got the right to vote.
1971 Eighteen-year-olds got the right to vote.
1990

1. Presidents (live) White House

   Presidents have lived in the White House since 1800.

2. Women (vote)

   ____

3. People (travel) transcontinental railroads

   ____

4. Ships (travel) Panama Canal

   ____

5. Eighteen-year-olds (vote)

   ____

6. People (pay) income taxes

   ____

Name ______________________________

Write your own feelings.

Write your own saying or paragraph about what the United States of America means to you. Use some of the words from the Word Bank if you wish.

Word Bank	
democracy	laws
equality	opportunity
fairness	responsibilities
freedom	rights
immigrant	voting

Name ______________________________

Words to Know

Find these words in the puzzle. Circle them.

AMENDMENT
AMERICA
BILL OF RIGHTS
CONGRESS
HOUSE
LEGISLATIVE
PRESIDENT
SEPARATION OF POWERS
SENATE
SUPREME COURT
VOTE

J	P	R	O	S	F	G	D	X	T	B	U	S	L	X	V	F	C
K	R	V	X	D	A	X	B	H	S	C	D	J	G	T	P	K	D
S	E	P	A	R	A	T	I	O	N	O	F	P	O	W	E	R	S
E	S	T	M	X	M	F	L	M	D	N	K	L	T	M	O	LO	U
A	I	O	E	U	E	B	L	H	V	G	H	T	E	C	V	K	P
D	D	N	N	M	R	G	O	L	T	R	I	G	H	T	S	A	R
A	E	X	D	G	I	D	F	X	X	E	P	B	C	G	K	N	E
K	N	P	M	H	C	P	R	L	H	S	E	N	A	T	E	H	M
C	T	N	E	U	A	E	I	G	C	S	M	T	J	X	S	U	E
F	H	M	N	I	A	B	G	K	O	N	X	E	H	L	D	C	C
A	V	O	T	E	U	K	H	O	U	S	E	O	X	M	T	X	O
S	T	L	X	F	T	D	T	O	S	B	U	V	L	J	H	V	U
M	V	C	L	E	G	I	S	L	A	T	I	V	E	N	T	U	R
K	X	U	B	S	L	V	N	F	N	X	D	C	H	F	A	B	T

Name ____________________

Consonant Blends

Complete each word in the sentences below, using *fl, br, dr, pr, st,* or *sp.*

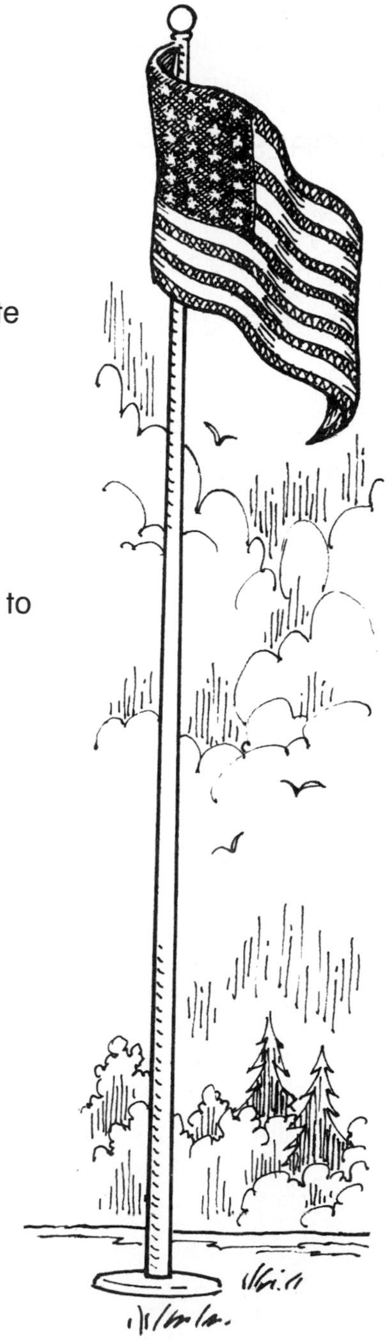

1. The U.S. ______ag has 13 stripes and 50 ______ars.

2. ______ags ______ap when there is a ______eeze.

3. The ______atue of Liberty ______ands in New York Harbor.

4. The ______esident of the United ______ates lives in the White House.

5. Congress is the legislative ______anch of government.

6. Congress is the ______anch of government that decides how to ______end the government's money.

7. ______udents should ______ udy about the history of the United States.

8. New citizens ______omise to obey the laws of the land.

9. One ______ecial holiday is ______esidents' Day. It honors Washington and Lincoln.

10. Many immigrants came to the United States to fulfill their ______eams.

Name ______________________________

Social Studies Objective: Demonstrate an understanding of civic values and rights and responsibilities of American citizenship.

Clues

1. When you take tests, many questions will ask you to analyze the main political, economic, and social ideas in the United States.
2. Other questions will deal with the effects of civic participation and the balance of civic rights.

Samples

1. If conflicts between laws occur,

   A. the President decides the law

   B. courts decide the law

   C. all the laws are ignored

   D. people decide the law

B is the correct answer. Courts decide on laws.

2. Under the original Constitution, representatives were the only government officials

   A. allowed to make laws

   B. represented in Washington

   C. elected directly by qualified voters

   D. registered to vote

The correct response is C.

Name ______________________________

Try It

Read each question. Mark the circle next to the correct answer.

1. A description of the basic laws and principles of a group is called
   - ○ a government
   - ○ a declaration
   - ○ a Bill of Rights
   - ○ a constitution

2. Changes to the United States Constitution are called
   - ○ revisions
   - ○ rewrites
   - ○ amendments
   - ○ new laws

3. The legislative branch of the United States that makes laws is called
   - ○ the Bill of Rights
   - ○ the Congress
   - ○ the CIA
   - ○ the Pentagon

4. Which of these is NOT a requirement for voting in most county, city, state, and national elections?
   - ○ Income
   - ○ Age
   - ○ Citizenship

Word Log

Word Log

Word Log